A MID-LIFE PERSPECTIVE: CONVERSATIONS WITH THE UNCONSCIOUS

A Subjective Study of Science, Religion, and Consciousness

ISBN-13: 978-1496090584

CONTENTS

LIST OF ILLUSTRATIONS

To Debra, the love of my life, to my daughter, Holly, and to all future generations who will be drawn inexorably to confront the mystery of the unconscious psyche.

The psychic background modern culture has repressed
By mythic mysteries alone can be expressed.
They point to depths the conscious mind can only see
But indirectly through its dream-like imagery.

Preface

More and more people today feel a lack of meaning in traditional religious values. Thousands of years of devotion which once found us praying for salvation are distant relics to the priorities of modern thought. The old metaphysical view has little in common with an increasingly scientific outlook fastened onto the material world.

The swing toward natural reality from earlier preoccupations with the spiritual realm has produced a body of facts so opposed to religious faith that the moral and ethical principles of just a generation ago are now recognizable in name only. As new clashes with old, the quest for knowledge obscures the need for wisdom.

Centuries of spiritual idealism which sought to develop the soul have instead convinced us that we have only to believe in it to achieve it – for those who can still believe. For those who can't, a new ideal of material progress now discards the too-taxing task of looking inward as not worth the effort.

Media-driven thing-obsession and near compulsive consumption divert vital energies. Ever more advanced technologies draw us further outside ourselves and into devices. Instant access and constant exposure to the subliminal effects of marketing and advertising cultivate unconscious emotions so paradoxical that what is meant to emancipate and connect also finds us dependent and alienated -- our most personal and intimate needs indistinguishable from carefully instilled, pre-packed desires.

A struggling clergy, unable to translate the older values into contemporary terms, cannot defend its views in the face of rational argument. Literally interpreted, religious symbols not only don't make sense to a science based on observable facts, they appear ridiculous and even silly. Worn half-truths and a declining relevance find modern mega-churches resorting to the same impersonal strategies driving business and political interests: mass commercial appeal. Science and religion have become adversaries competing for consumers; the individual, an insignificant statistic buried under the anonymity of target groups, market niches, and sales pitches.

I first perceived these anxieties as personal problems. I felt that something was missing in my life, sensed only as vague needs somehow opposed to my intentions. Seeking clarity, I turned to the psychological studies of C.G. Jung and his colleague, Erich Neumann. With the aid of Jung's model, I began to understand that my feelings also reflected deeper conflicts beneath our assumptions of who we are and how we see our place in the natural world. As the religious view fades and the scientific one replaces it, an uneasy apprehension steals behind a facade of certainty.

A major shift in perspective accompanies today's fast-paced super-highways of information. Jung's and Neumann's comparative studies of consciousness revealed patterns -- evolutionary swings in its focus throughout history. They saw such shifts as reflections of unconscious organizing and centering functions. Their purpose is to re-orient us at certain critical stages to the more diffuse aims of spiritual and psychological development. Until recently, those aims were the province of religion and philosophy. That has changed. The beginning of the new stage is marked by a revolutionary discovery in the trend toward objective inquiry: the old metaphysical images proved to be the symbolic language of an unconscious psyche.

The discovery and its implications are largely ignored. The dark past of our moral history then opened to deeper scrutiny instead sees modern sensibilities rejecting the new knowledge. The grounds for its denial are not far to seek: this latest swing toward technology bodes a frightening new confrontation with our destructive tendencies. The repressed anxiety sensed by ego at an in-depth inspection of itself finds the old fear of God still alive beneath our diversions – and with good reason.

In *The Origins and History of Consciousness*, Erich Neumann described this shift in values: "Typical and symptomatic of this transitional phenomenon is the state of affairs in America, though the same holds good for practically the whole Western hemisphere... The grotesque fact that murderers, brigands, thieves, forgers, tyrants, and swindlers, in a guise that deceives nobody, have seized control of collective life is characteristic of our time. Their unscrupulousness and double-dealing are recognized -- and admired. Their ruthless energy they obtain at best from some stray archetypal content that has got them in its power. The dynamism of a possessed personality is accordingly very great, because in its one-track primitivity, it suffers none of the differentiations which make men human."

Neumann published his book in 1954, when the spectacles of Nazism and Hiroshima were recent events; when humanity was gravely concerned about its future amid the nuclear destruction which burst through the veil of civilization. We have since been lulled into a trance by the glitter of a far more complex and pervasive technology, even as military motives yet work in secrecy behind it. Neumann:

"Worship of the "beast" is not confined to Germany; it prevails wherever one-sidedness, push, and moral blindness are applauded, i.e., wherever the aggravating complexities of civilized behavior are swept away by bestial rapacity. One has only to look at the educative ideals current in the West. The possessed character of our financial and industrial magnates... is psychologically evident from the very fact that they are at the mercy of a suprapersonal factor – "work," "power," "money," or whatever they like to call it – which in the telling phrase "consumes" them and leaves little or no room as private persons. Coupled with a nihilistic attitude toward civilization there goes a puffing up of the ego-sphere which expresses itself with brutish egotism in a total disregard for the common good..."

Neumann outlined the social effects of this transition: "Not only power, money, and lust, but religion, art, and politics as exclusive determinants in the form of parties, sects, movements, and "isms" of every description take possession of the masses and destroy the individual."

The emotional confusion generated by such a major shift in values is only enhanced today by a profound lack of introspection. The "suprapersonal factors" embodied in religious images are intended to orient us inwardly; to center and protect us from being swept away by mass contagion. Our ideas of religion are changing, and there is no return to the old ways. Deep in the throes of unseen psychic forces, consciousness is being pushed in a new direction. The possibilities for further development hidden in the older ideas require a re-interpretation of the peculiar language of the depth from which they spring and the symbols it produces.

An important distinction must be made between sign and symbol: Jung defined a symbol as an image of the unknown. A sign stands for something known; it contains only the information we have put into it. Symbols evoke unconscious complexes of ideas which draw us to their many possible meanings and our relation to them. Just as science is concerned primarily with a concrete world of objects, religious images, too, are viewed as "things" containing only the beliefs that have been put into them, interpreting them more literally as signs than symbols.

Self-awareness means to perceive the inner world as well as the outer one. The one-sidedness of our current rational trend, a reaction to the religious view, has resulted in a new extreme in focus. To think logically, intellect must repress emotion; to the degree that we identify with it, we are at odds with ourselves. The over-reliance on one function to the exclusion of others is a threat to our psychic balance. The unconscious attempts to restore equilibrium by creating circumstances through unintended and "accidental" consequences which form an inner counter-pole to conscious direction: the basis of the tension of opposites, their relativity, and the swings produced by changes from within.

Because a limited will only partially creates our conditions, the deeper effects of our actions are shrouded by the veil of conscious intent. We also react to inner circumstances which are just as real as the outer ones, unseen by the fascination with the sensual and concrete. What we see and what we can't see are determined by the concepts which shape our perceptions. A different conceptual view is required to grasp the effects of the psychic reality we can't see: a symbolic one.

These ideas are the general concerns of this book. They describe the analogical thinking needed to bridge the divide between the scientific and religious views – the two ends of a psychic spectrum which determine how we see ourselves and the world. Their comparison is an important step in understanding the diversions and obsessions which have us in their hold; to reduce the severity in the swings of the pendulum between our dual natures. As cultural institutions, these viewpoints are obstinate to change, and nature seeks development through the creative responses of the individual. Group conflicts originate in the individual, and the opposed forces defining them can only be confronted and resolved there.

The text describes this confrontation in terms of the individuation process as conceived by Jung. His research confirms the mid-life process as the emergence of a more personal, inward call to self than the social orientation of the first half. Its purpose is to deepen relations with the spiritual functions which have always guided us. They are synonymous with development, and coming to terms with them today is an individual problem. Once the herd instinct takes over and fixes onto an ideal, it remains static; only individuals are capable of introducing new perceptions of it.

Though the book revolves around the mid-life experience, the continuity of development prepares it long before its intrusion into consciousness. In the first half, as we adapt to social conditions, a relatively dormant individuality is repressed in favor of cultural demands. The repressions accumulate over the initial stages, gaining energy until they form a complex of problems. We are then confronted with what the earlier view was not conditioned to see: the psychic reality behind appearances. This process creates an expanding spiral of evolution, and it follows the same guiding pattern in the individual, in condensed form, as in the history of the species.

Jung conceived this cycle as a re-adaptation, on progressively higher levels, to the spirit: the dark, unconscious life-energy driving material existence. Under the pressure of this urge to orient us to the inner world, ego begins to feel its identity emerge through a different lens than the worldly scope which shaped its beginnings. It is a change in perspective, analogous to the cultural one today, which reveals that previous values may be relative – not in legal terms of right and wrong but in relation to the history of development and the changing needs of an evolving consciousness.

Beneath our scientific preoccupations, we remain in the stage of psychological awareness reflected in our religious heritage. Behind the curtain of moral judgment lurk the split figures of good and evil: a model of how we relate to our unconscious natures. Jung has described how those ideas reflect the positive and negative poles necessary to produce psychic energy: the sliding scale along which consciousness fluctuates in its on-going efforts to define itself. Just as it forms the path of collective history, so in the growth of the individual in the first half of life, the repression of the unconscious required for ego to strengthen and develop now creates circumstances which signal the need for a new relation to it -- to balance conscious direction; to relate it, make it relative to the counter-pole of inner development.

This book is a chronicle in poetic form of my own mid-life transition. It spans sixteen years of effort to understand the ideas conveyed in my dreams. Poetry seemed best suited to express my emotional conflicts, and I wrote down my meditations as the material shaped itself. Certain themes began to stand out; patterns emerged as I gave voice to the unconscious through three figures representing the spiritual and psychological demands urged upon me.

The text is comprised of a kind of dialectic, an exchange of ideas, between those three figures and a fourth representing consciousness. In that sense, the material is not mine; I tried to give expression to the process as it formed in me. I followed the unconscious directives without preconception as to where they might lead, allowing them as far as possible to create their own picture. The result was both a story and an example, an analogy, of Jung's model: a description of how psychic energy flows toward unconscious aims through the elaboration of ideas.

As I used the third person, *The Ancient King* emerged as the director of the instinctive urge toward wholeness. He embodies the innate drive to connect us with the religious and philosophical history of who we are beneath our assumptions. *The Dark Prince* personifies the shadowy intuitions intended to push consciousness to a deeper interpretation of its nature. Those reflections gradually penetrate the collective emotional world of *The Unknown Woman*. *The Oddly Shaped Man* is the ego-standpoint as it struggles to comprehend the confusion created by their demands.

To make the text more understandable, several themes must be borne in mind regarding these unconscious demands as the poem proceeds. I have highlighted them for those who may want to refer back to them as they follow their progression:

The Human Animal

Civilization is a comparatively recent product when weighed against the immense stretch of time required for consciousness to emerge from the depths of instinctual nature. The beast tokens our animal ancestry, and the eons-long climb through the darkness of pre-history yet finds it just below the threshold of culture. As a symbol, it relates not only to our biological heritage through the body and its functions but to our sense of individuality, as it is through our bodies that we first experience ourselves as distinct and separate from others.

As humanity developed, the snake in the Garden evolved into Satan in the Old Testament, and both symbolize the opposition needed to distinguish conscious from unconscious. Each toddler repeats this contrary "no" stage in its development, and that opposition is a vital factor in the growth and consolidation of consciousness. It is a basic conflict between a "god-like" self-awareness set against a split-off instinctual heritage. The horns and tail of the Devil later became a graphic description of the animal urges repressed for their gradual conversion into the more humanizing social instincts embraced by Christian ideals.

As the newer myth took hold, the spiritual aim of building the soul, the personal relation to the Deity, sank beneath the weight of a still-developing and over-compensating collective ego, emphasizing the long, serpentine conflicts required for individual evolution. Psychologically and spiritually, ego-effects are a gauge of self-knowledge. Despite centuries of religious exhortation, they remain in much the same state now as in the past. The writer, Philip Wylie, described this idea as "the fatuous awe of the ape with the mirror." The ape points not only to a stunted inner life but to regressive tendencies which both conceal and reveal the psychological dawn of those who would recognize and act upon their own inner opposition.

Nature and the Unconscious

This theme revolves around the image of the earth as a natural symbol of the unconscious. The earth and sun are the sources of all known life, suitable metaphors for the masculine and feminine forces which conceive it. Jung and Neumann have demonstrated that artifacts and symbols dating back to pre-patriarchal cultures intimately associate masculinity with light and consciousness, just as feminine images are associated with unconscious darkness and fertility: the earthly and the feminine, the creative matrix which bears and fosters the child of consciousness. Symbolically, masculinity refers to the heady principles of thought, the organizing of consciousness; the feminine principle dissolves separate tendencies to form emotional and physical relationships – properties of the soul.

The primitive mind long ago conceived the sun as spirit, reflecting processes which urged the coming of light to the dark, unconscious void of human origin. Earth and sun are psychological analogues for "feminine" relatedness -- the oneness of the unconscious, the body, and the individual -- and the dissecting, masculine character of consciousness. Together, they express the intermingling pairs of opposites and the penetrating form of their relationship. Male and female, spirit and matter, mind and body: all describe the two poles required for conscious orientation.

Primitive sun-worship anticipated a Christian myth "not of this world". Both signify the urge to distinguish conscious from unconscious, just as it is repeated in the individual. The movement away from nature toward an artificial fantasy-sphere is a projection of over-extension. Jung and Neumann suggested that the natural process of separating the two psychic systems has deepened into such a division today that we can no longer relate to our instinctual foundations – a kind of collective mid-life change in the centering and organizing processes of the psyche. Our intellectual inflation only accentuates our historical opposition to nature and the corresponding functions designed to relate us to earthly reality.

As the momentum of this drive toward conscious identity finds us alienated from ourselves, the unconscious attempts to re-orient us in the current swing by steering us back to itself, to nature and the earth, to our physical/emotional ground. The swing toward natural science describes a symbolic movement. The spiritual unfolding of our natures speaks only indirectly through its own language.

The creative spirit turns destructive when it is restricted to conscious aims and remains unconscious for too long, when a new stage is signaled. Our systematic abuse of the earth reveals an inner conflict: the oscillating poles of spirit and matter seek the undeveloped functions still in the sway of the old stage. The artificial environment we have created in the relatively short swing back to the material world exposes our Christian disdain for nature as a symbol of our animal heritage and a "god-like" ego which cannot accept its origins or its subjection to natural laws. We are literally poisoning ourselves and our children, even as exaggerated fantasies pursue grandiose notions of "conquering" space -- still driven by an inflated and unanchored ego which sees itself as "not of this world."

Ego and Intellect

The identification of ego with intellect contributes to this problematic conception of nature. It long slumbered in Christian theology as identification with an otherworldly God and a disdain for natural life: an image of self-rejection – one of the reasons guilt weighs so heavily in traditional religious ideas. Both are compounded through this identity, the idea of a Deity now yielding to science as it dissolves the metaphysical projections. For all our rational knowledge, we remain driven by the repressed "natural man" who serves the sensual world of material desire – just as he did many thousands of years ago. He personifies the unconscious need for a wider psychological perspective than just an intellectual one – and the internal guilt we never came to terms with because we never understood the reasons for it.

The uneven advance of self-knowledge finds no adequate ideas that would relate us to the ancient symbols and their functions, their irrational truths repressed for lack of understanding. They sink back into the unconscious where they become hostile adversaries. Due to changes in consciousness, they resurface in different guise today, though we remain possessed by their "suprapersonal" powers – paradoxically more distant now than ever. As our relation to ourselves is no longer expressed in the old images, the humbling effects of a higher authority dwindle into vague personal beliefs with no real emotional experience to support them. The result is a "puffing up of the ego-sphere" and the "brutish egotism" to which Neumann referred: an exaggerated urge to individuality which has lost its relation to itself and the world.

From the scientific perspective, religious images are only fantasies. For the less developed intellect of the past, they served to influence thought's exclusive tendencies. The objective trend today requires a new interpretation of the values they represent. The conflicts of the soul, the emotional tensions determining our deepest relations in the context of a greater whole, are projected onto fractional interests and ideologies with ever more threatening consequences.

Only the hard work of introspection can free the individual from the self-flattering and contradictory influences of ego. The recognition of a higher inner authority beyond will and intellect is a philosophical and religious process meant to bind us to humanity and our natural environment. For science to serve those greater purposes, its aims must be subject to a broader conception of psychic life.

Causality and Purpose

The causal thinking which orients our perception is opposed to the heavy, symbolic language of the unconscious. The one leads backward in time to a cause that produces effects, and the other leads forward to a purpose or goal without conceiving a cause. As a concept, the latter allows the thoughts, feelings, and intuitions evoked by images and symbols to shape themselves; to relate their associations to the pursuit of aims beyond conscious preconception.

Jung saw the idea of time as a primitive concept of energy, a gradient of potential, in that it flows forward in an irreversible way. This is an approximate analogy for his model of psychic energy and the reason time is capitalized in the text when referred to by the figures representing the unconscious. We can reverse it in our minds as in casual thought, but we should be aware that we are projecting subjective ideas onto the objective behavior of processes outside consciousness.

Each individual sees the world a little differently according to his/her personal interpretations: Jung's "subjective factor". He stressed that it is "one of the necessary conditions under which all thinking takes place." We may agree on certain general ways of thinking, but this in no way relieves them of their subjective quality. It is conscious thought which subjectivizes the ideas we associate. The historical advance from collective thinking to individual differentiation accentuates this subjective influence. The tendency toward specialization and the proliferation of "isms" attests this movement. Though still veiled by symbolic mythical influences, the undeveloped seeds of individuality are gradually emerging through the dense fog of collective history – or at least attempting to.

The opposition between causal thought and the forward movement of the unconscious, along with the projection of subjective viewpoints, create contradictions in our thinking. When looking inward, one of the most perplexing ones is the backward flow of dream-images as they draw on past experience. This paradox reflects the double meaning inherent in unconscious imagery, just as it is the basis of the causal view. The opposites are still fused together in the unconscious; it is the discriminating effect of consciousness that splits the original image and reveals only the partial aspect of its focus. Only the two forms of perceiving combined can give us a wider sense of who we are beneath our one-sided presumptions.

Past, present, and future are a single dynamic process in the unconscious. One of the functions of dreams is to express this creative flow through analogies with present circumstances. Since analogies describe how different sets of experiences conform, dreams often express immediate concerns through memory-images. They reveal the conformities of past and present events, our reactions to them, and the anticipations of tendencies which shape our futures. Jung stated: "Everything psychic is pregnant with the future."

Religious Images

Because it consists of a living history of our mental functioning, Jung wrote that any serious inquiry into the unconscious leads straight into the religious problem. This theme fully emerges in the second part of the book. As the poem proceeds, the intuitive side of religious ideas is explored. Job was the older anticipation of the individual who confronts the collective background to discover his or her own way; in so doing, a dialogue is entered into with the unconscious.

Job had achieved the material tasks of the first part of life. His faith, his connection to the Deity, was then tested through Jehovah's bargain with Satan. The bargain represents the interplay of opposites: the deeper unconscious process which precedes awareness. Job's sufferings comprised the circumstances which compelled him to reflect on, to make conscious, this inner exchange. According to the analogies of that time, Job's afflictions were depicted physically; today we would interpret them as projections of psychic conflicts. If we take the concrete qualities out of the figures and translate them into ideas, as we might attempt to do with our dreams, we can begin to see how they analogize psychic processes.

When we reflect on these stories, we may grasp their symbolic meanings by relating them to our own emotional conditions. Christ, as the Son of Man, was a later anticipation of development; an ideal image of the individual which emerged from the spiritual darkness and brutality of antiquity for the purpose of further transforming our animal natures. His crucifixion is a powerful analogy of the tension of psychic opposites encountered by one who turns inward, away from the material world, and begins to discern his/her personal values apart from prevailing views.

As with Job, it is no coincidence that the myth of Christ revolved around his crucifixion at the mid-life point. Today, the spiritual changes reflected in the tasks of individuation stand, too, as a prototype of development in a new age. Just as these tasks make demands on those compelled to confront them, so they reverberate in the collective unconscious. Psychic reality is coming to bear on our times.

Alchemy

Jung's devotion to the study of alchemy was an attempt to illustrate it as a connective stage between our historical religious outlook and the emerging scientific one. Alchemy was the intermediate form of the two views that later diverged. Like those of theology, alchemical ideas were psychic projections, though less collectively developed and therefore more expressive of natural tendencies.

As a science, alchemy paved the way to our modern conception of the world, but as a philosophy it expressed the very ideas missing in a one-sided Christianity: the problem of opposition between spirit and nature; the "evil" of the material world, of the repressed feminine and its dark urge toward a re-orientation to matter – to Mother Earth and the body and all that the patriarchal myth rejected. Alchemy connected to the inner counter-pole intended to balance and direct a distorted conscious view.

Jung's work parallels alchemical philosophy in that he sought a symbolic solution to the unconscious conflicts they represent today. The soul is a fact of emotional experience, a psychic reality. It can be seen as a natural function if we have some understanding of symbols. The symbolic view relies as much on feeling and intuition as thinking. For the intellectual standpoint, feeling is the opposed function designed to balance its orientation. The blinding of inner perception by an increasing outer-direction suggests the repression of confusion which occurs in any shift in perspective. Coming to terms with the soul means the development of emotions which would supplement the "masculine" rational viewpoint and relate it to the greater value of goals beyond its narrow focus.

The themes highlighted above are the core ideas of this book, and they carry something of the form of unconscious language with them. The analogies elaborating it are more circular than linear. Associations throng around the ideas to be explained as they compel attention, gradually becoming clearer with increased concentration. Images weave around and through one another to form deeper connections as they thread their opposing tendencies toward a uniform flow.

The compensating nature of the unconscious revolves around an objective organizing function which is presupposed, not only in dreams but in all natural processes. A subjective consciousness is filled out by its circular complexes of ideas; the urge to wholeness gives us a rounder and more complete picture of an inner reality which is just as objective as the outer one.

Though the ego is only one complex of associations in the psyche, it has evolved as a coordinator: what it is drawn to as an object of attention will be where and how its energy is applied. These motives are based on unconscious processes, and only by turning conscious attention to them can we find deeper meaning and purpose beyond the preconceptions of ego and its one-sided, paradoxical intentions.

It is in the old alchemical spirit in which this book was written. It is an acknowledgment of the unconscious as it seeks to compensate the modern tendencies which have evolved through our history. Our scientific thinking has plucked a new fruit from the old Tree of Knowledge. To understand its effects, intellect must be applied as a tool for understanding what we do, not as a blind end in itself.

This entails not only a therapeutic approach back to ourselves through the introspection of our historical roots but forward to a new spiritual possibility which can accept the earthly, the feminine, and the animal aspects of our natures. The problems facing us today will not be solved by technology – it is a perilous diversion. We need psychological knowledge to understand the creative/destructive movements of the unconscious; some form of subjective truth to begin the inner dialectic which would lead us to a sense of responsibility which modern values increasingly lack. Our future calls us to look at the beast of psychic regression and its demands below the threatening complexities of technology.

Beyond my own predicament, I have known many who have been swallowed up by the mid-life process – think of Jonah and the whale. Today, it takes the form of alcoholism, drug addiction, and/or a dark, consuming world of depression and compulsive behavior. Without a spiritual perspective and an understanding of psychic law, we remain adrift in a vast sea of contradictory images vying for our attention. Culture teaches us nothing about an inner transition; the individual is important to it only insofar as it can be exploited to support itself.

The underlying tension of the individual's relation to culture, however, is a fundamental conflict of psychic life, a catalyst for development from infancy to old age. If the individual cannot discern him/herself apart from these impersonal forces, he/she is unconsciously carried along by them, and this herding effect only magnifies the dangerous potential of mass movements. All unconscious conflicts have a dual nature: subjective and objective, personal and social, creative and destructive. Their opposing tendencies converge in the psyche, and they determine our actions. How we perceive and evaluate them will decide our future. In the wake of World War II, Jung wrote: "The world hangs on a thin thread; that thread is the psyche of man. How important is it to know something about it?"

The illustrations are enigmatic. In fact, they were as nearly confusing to me as they may appear to others. They are essentially dream-images, and they "formed themselves" as I lent my pen to them, just as I later followed the promptings of the figures comprising the unconscious voice in the conversations. They emerged in an intense period of concentration at the beginning of my efforts to understand Jung's work and are dispersed throughout the book at intervals which seemed to me to best fit the ideas associated with them. They are symbolic representations of future development, and the book is an elaboration of the ideas they contain. As dream-images, they do not lend themselves to rational explanation. They are pointers of the way which express the feelings and intuitions beyond thought and logic.

I would like to share one final note concerning the history of symbols and its practical value in the life of the individual. The image of the round black dot, the subject of the Prologue, appeared to me in a dream when I was a very young child. In it, my focus was drawn to the horizon where it hung suspended like a small planet just above it. It remained a profound curiosity throughout my life, and I reflected often on its possible meaning to no avail.

As I became immersed in the study of Jung's work at age forty, I found that it was the member of a family of symbols well known in the history of philosophy and religion. I read of a medieval alchemist whose dream depicted that same black dot hanging above the horizon, just as I saw it in mine. The old Greek atom is a similar idea and referred psychologically to qualities of indivisibility and wholeness. Gnostic thought conceived it as the indivisible point; alchemy, as the soul-spark.

The Greek historian, Hippolytus, in his documentation of Gnostic ideas in the second century A.D., described this indivisible point: "This point, being nothing and consisting of nothing, attains a magnitude incomprehensible by thought... this mustard seed which grows into the kingdom of God." It hints at the blackness, the unconscious density and irrationality of life-processes which exceed explanation.

At that point in my life I was very rationally oriented. My view of religion was critical, indeed -- though I was soon struck by its emotional implications. The historical meaning of this symbol put my dream into a spiritual context I would not otherwise have known -- the purpose of the unconscious counter-pole: I discovered that, even though I was consciously anti-religious, my deeper nature flowed along powerful spiritual undercurrents. Without that basic knowledge, I was in constant contradiction with myself. Unaware of their meaning, the conflicts of development could only appear as obstacles outside.

Like Paul's conversion on the road to Damascus, that insight awakened the mid-life process and allowed it to emerge into consciousness. It gave new purpose to my life and a sense of the value of spiritual orientation. My conflict with the religious view was with traditional interpretations, as it is with many thinking people today. I know that all have such dreams as can be accessed through Jung's work -- the reason I was compelled to share my experiences. The unconscious psyche, that dark and unknown entity within, has an animal as well as a god-like character. To repress its dual reality is to deny the most vital and creative parts of our natures.

Evan Hanks

2014

DEDICATION

To the great pagan poet I owe more than I can say
Who long ago endeavored with the most profound command
To face the opposition in his heart and then portray
With such grace and wisdom his reflections on the soul of man.
Centuries have passed away beyond his own emprise;
Yet his poetry ignited in my modern heart
An ancient mystery those centuries cannot revise
Nor even future histories the minds of men may chart.
The beauty of his flowing verse, the pain between the lines;
His acceptance of the knowing curse of dark despair
Afflicting those of men on earth the spirit so inclines
Found me parched and thirsting my own spirit to declare.
It was the last great myth a human soul produced:
This bargain with the Devil in the depths of men;
For the minds of men before and long since have seduced
That same Devil to replace this task within.
It stands as an image to our modern thought today
For those who worship idols of the mind's extremes:
Whether to an ancient god or science they might pray
These idols in the minds of men are distant dreams
Until they have the courage to accept the task
To look inside and see behind the idol's mask.
It was the German Faust conceived in this creative role
In Goethe's mind: the pagan poet of the human soul.

Prologue

The idea of wholeness is introduced through the image of the round black dot. The psychic background of this ancient symbol which is to be examined, developed, and integrated into consciousness is outlined. It symbolizes the life-energy behind all natural development; an idea which is presupposed in the wider concept of evolution – even in scientific theories of the origins of the universe. Its psychological/spiritual significance is hinted at in the biblical idea: it is the mustard seed of dormant individuality, the deeper self. Jung called it a "complexio oppositorum": a dark, unknown core of potential, the undifferentiated opposites of future discrimination. It is an archetypal nature-symbol pre-dating traditional religious ones, but like them it anticipates a conscious orientation to the spirit-world of the unconscious.

THE ANCIENT KING.

    In the dawn of life a dream to him I sent:

    His own spirit's vision of his fate unfurled.

    It echoes in his consciousness the dark intent

    Seizing now upon his artificial world.

    It was a scene so vivid and alive

    For half his life it managed to survive;

    And now to such a magnitude it shall attain

    His intellect shall only seek for it in vain.

    For, access to this living image in his soul

    Is only found through Nature's own fantastic goal.

    It was a glimpse into the infinite

    That preordained the voice he hears;

    For, the mystery condensed in it

    Has kept him linked to spirit-spheres --

    Bound him fast in his inmost bcing

Though year upon year all spirit fleeing.

He felt then the frightening wondrous reach

Of a world beyond the boundaries of speech.

His undeveloped mind at once was hurled

Tiny and scared through this natural world.

But only for the fraction of an hour --

Only later would he feel its greater power...

This secret of his soul in its design

Was only meant to hint at the divine;

For he was destined first to have his fill

Of the mundane life his youth conceived as real.

Only now at mid-life with his youth gone by

Shall he need this dream that graced his infant eye.

For those whose natures it shall befit

As on stone tablets it has been writ:

The round was prized in antiquity --

For this man too shall it likewise be.

How shall one small man such burdens shoulder

But through conflicts he endured as he grew older?

Of men's illusions he has had a humbling share;

They've inspired him to seek for answers elsewhere.

He's been provided what he needs as he requires

But not 'til need is great shall he acknowledge these desires.

The artificial sun of man however bright

At last shall find him lost and blinded by the sight.

Without this fight he would remain perversely young

And the song of Nature's mystery have died unsung...

Thus is he afflicted with a burden he must bear

Though until he owns it he shall suffer unaware;

For the symbols of this burden are of such a kind
As to evade the comprehension of a younger mind.
The round black dot of antiquity is at its root;
And though the trials of youth were always hidden there
Just as Nature's seeds contain the image of the fruit
The later more developed and mature tree shall bear
This image long has guided him in his pursuit
Whose meaning only older riper years prepare.
Indeed he stands upon the cusp of youth and age
Compelled to seek this symbol of a later stage.
His soul has signaled this new struggle to begin:
He must bear the burden of this older man within.
The fuel for such a spirit-process is provided
By the clash of energies his own thought divided.
The feeling part his youthful mind rejected
Shall soon emerge through functions long projected...

Part I

Confrontation with the Unconscious

Dethronement of the Ego

The Mid-life Process

The mid-life transition begins with a confusing influx of unconscious emotional demands. It supplements the one-sided perspective of causal thinking by exposing its inadequacies in confronting the inner world. This re-orienting phase is marked by changing relationships as the growing insistence of the unconscious begins to intrude in the form of repressed feelings. The images attending this stage are often of a sexual character, symbolizing the creative life-urge of the unconscious, as well as the motive forces of instinctual functions which are more emotional than sensual. Psychologically, Jung saw sexuality as a function of relationship. Studies of primates suggest that promiscuous sexual activities within the group serve the purpose of social cohesion. These are the dark beginnings of culture. On a higher level, the dual nature of mind and body serves a similar role within the psyche as the two poles seeking a gradient for spiritual development: the deeper shift in values that occurs between them at mid-life.

THE DARK PRINCE.

  Cast to the flames of a sacrificial fire --
  Nakedness, crudeness in unholy choir --
  The spirit of Nature with Time will conspire
  To turn into ashes her own desire.
  The animal's heated moan is heard
  Deep in the body unconsciously stirred
  With lust to entice the intimate vice
  Of the apple of Eden's sacrifice;
  Fixed to an image his youth has crowned --
  Still to a primitive energy bound.

The pretense of love dissolves and emerges

As frantic obsessions with sexual urges

Embracing another in secret fashion

Transfusing his own with the other's passion.

Idols undressed in an intimate tryst

Are clothed in the dream of the image he kissed;

Obscured by the lure of the heightened need

To transcend himself in the concrete deed.

Selfishness grows into frenzied caprice

Unconsciously seeking the Spirit's release.

His naked desire is then transformed

Into an object erotic, deformed;

Conceived as need in a sensual feast

Of animal functions exposed and released.

Nakedness glows as a sumptuous sight

Devoid of love and impelled by the might

Of a ravenous ravishing appetite

Consuming his senses in crude delight...

Bedazzled by erotic fascination --

Yet in the animal stage of creation --

He's forced in his darkness to yield all control

To this secret excitement concealed in his soul.

Ribbons of touch flow over his skin

Alluring and hazy drawing him in.

Worlds of paradox dance before his eyes;

Earthly pleasures whisper and in the darkness lies

The secret co-conspirator in lusty grinning guise

Who barters sex for love through his compulsive ties.

Passion's loneliness seeks him out

From the desperate to the devout.

For many years he has fantasized

That the flesh should hide the gift he prized.

From urge to compulsion his mind has run;

Round and round have his senses spun

Blindly hoping to reach through the veil

To find a passion now grown pale;

Stripped of form by the inner eye

Ravaged by greed and left to die --

Then to be strewn in the dark expanse:

The seed of his nature in Time's advance;

Compelled by fate to fecundate

The fertile spirit who lies in wait.

The grin will vanish and through love's guise

A more discerning man will meet his eyes.

Will he in Faustian surprise salute

The higher nature of this lowly brute?

Or fan the flames of his naked desire;

Genuflect to the world of men

Admit his weakness before this fire

Confess the paradox and then –

Ignore the flame of fate within?

Whatever choice will not avail him long

For this dark voice will soon become too strong.

Where impulse, need, and fear ring round

Nature's urge to consciousness is found.

Has he the courage to implore

This demon-spirit in the dark?

Stripped of the manly clothes he wore

Confronted by a truth so stark?

Here is he at a strange frontier

Caught on the edge of aloneness and fear;

Destined by Nature and Time to explore

The unknown magic he sought before:

His naked desire where once did glow

The secret excitement he longs to know.

THE UNKNOWN WOMAN.

A new relation with himself he now must seek;

Before this task the strongest will proves small and weak.

However much his nakedness has fascinated

A deeper image of his life will be created.

If the images he seeks at night engender love

Whence come the feelings daylight finds him thinking of?

The secret needs his lonely lust allays at night

Soon will find him subject to another appetite.

Ever in his naked pleasure, strive as strive he may

Passion's night though darkly veiled must labor into day.

The fleet relations with the needs he fantasizes

On the plate of pleasure Nature's power now disguises

Are appetizers for a different reality --

Ones when savored will consume him too as he will see.

While he sits starving now at the same old table

For the same old dish warmed over by his fantasy --

Only by the spice of fantasy made edible --

Youth's repast must yield at last for spirit's truths to free.

What fare has he yet tasted whose illusory appeal

Did not later seize him with the pain of indigestion?

He finds another place to eat and eats the same old meal --

Though why it never sits quite right is loathe to question.

THE ODDLY SHAPED MAN.

Has a dark shadow dissipated?

Is this the image I created?

With my own seed did I propagate

This fog of illusion -- can this be fate?

THE ANCIENT KING.

That such unsaintly savageries should lurk

Where love's resplendent purposes unfold

Is at the very essence of the work –

A tale antiquity has long since told.

Eons before the mid-life sacrifice

The Son of Man embodied in this truth

Time and Nature used a similar device

To free the spirit from compulsive youth.

The dying and resurgent god of Nature

Was an image of the same analogy;

Now obscured by a modern nomenclature

But barely noted even by psychology.

The secret excitement conceals in his mind

An unconscious striving for orientation

To the two opposed powers discreetly entwined

In this mythical drama of mid-life creation.

Their double form is thought's discrimination

Of these opposites beneath its dark disguise;

And when in harmony with his cooperation

This narrow gate of grace reveals the secret prize.

The chief enigmas of this difficult art

Are the hidden snares of the human heart

The limited cast of the conscious light

And the magic illusion of its own sight.

Only love provokes the dread disease

Enticing men to labors such as these;

And in the end his nature shall decide

The value of the love he holds inside.

But Nature first initiates her plan

In a form attractive to a man.

In her willful way she shall ensure

A dark entanglement in this divine allure...

THE UNKNOWN WOMAN.

Such a lovely vision flowers from her presence --

So enchanting as she floats across the floor --

She reserves a certain silent reverence

Which impressed itself upon him all the more

By the way such loveliness emerges

Through the sweet affection sensed in every glance;

In the way her liquid eyes reflect his urges

To yield himself completely to her trance.

A touch would seem invasion of her lovely sphere

Even as her beauty whispers secret mysteries:

What would it be like to hold the shyness of a deer;

To kiss the fragrant essence of a summer's breeze?

For such a graceful air as stirs in any forest

To personify itself in woman's form

And reproduce such sweet melodic chorus

Is as moving as a springtime being born.

If the light of all of legend's sunrises

Could condense within a mythic pair of eyes;

Reveal the depth whose radiance disguises

The subtle character her loveliness belies

Then he could feel the magic of this creature

Who weaves her way through spirit's re-creation

To come alive in every mundane feature

So inviting in this lost preoccupation.

A secret sea of ancient energy exists

Within this image gravitating round;

Thronging, shoving, ever-longing it insists

Upon the living mystery to which it's bound.

Her aura hints at access to this world

Whose works are of such enigmatic source;

But where amid this captivating swirl

Does her own figure make itself a force?

It's the wider world of a deeper plea:

The waking dream of a new reality

Striving now to create and expand

A living relation to Nature's demand.

It pulls him whole within its vortex

Longingly and seeking to express

The coursing life concealed beneath his selfishness.

This little stream will soon release such torrents

As will flood the reaches of his stranded consciousness.

His pretensions will be swept away in currents

Too repressed and raging to allow control

To the flimsy screen of everyday existence

That veils the secret yearnings of his soul.

She drifts away with the intoxicating breeze

Of fleeting traces weaving wonder with her grace.

Dancing round before him with fascinating ease

Her fingers light a flame across his face...

THE ODDLY SHAPED MAN.

Did she spring from a nixie's dream within my mind?

Its lovely paradox aglow behind her smile?

Did Nature whisk me through this twilit view of time

As an omen of her oceanic style?

THE ANCIENT KING.

The path has been laid though it winding be;

Straight and narrow views lack deeper insight.

Who would imagine this mystery

Must feel the motion of Nature's might.

Back and forth she weaves her wayward course

To thread together two worlds separated;

That Nature's child be brought back to its source

And reconcile the spirit-world it abdicated.

The elemental force within this earthly race

Must have its source as well as an after-place:

This black circle symbolizes energy --

Whence it comes and whither it goes none may see.

The big-bang theory is derived from such a thought

Though strictly on the cosmic level it's been taught.

Matter is expanding out to breach a stellar night

The physicists insist in their obsessive view;

As if a god were modeled after human sight

And Nature would conform to its direction too.

Black holes must be theorized to compensate this urge;

An opposing force according to their thesis:

A dense abyss where even light cannot emerge --

A power with the pull to rend a god to pieces...

So image on image unceasingly create

Each form alluding to a man's internal state.

Still outward shall his heavens be expanding

When he perceives the need for inner understanding?

The most enigmatic riddles sent by me

Shall tax his head as if to burst asunder

To lead him to the place he needs to be

To feel the strength of all creation's wonder.

Indeed shall his head be rent in pieces

As Nature seeks to make her purpose known;

But over time to manifest a process

For years of struggle his illusions to atone.

In this task of tearing and destruction

He shall penetrate the essence of my name.

Far beneath the ruin of his world construction

He shall see the turbid glow of spirit's flame.

This flame is lit by Nature's *inner* mystery --

All but extinguished by the science of today.

An older science must reveal its darker history

Before his modern consciousness perceives its ray:

The black sun of alchemy was known to ancient men

And when a man discerns it he is on his own way.

It was the light the Christian glare consumed back then –
Now obscured by the sun of intellect to pray.
It illuminates the depth of a forgotten past:
The very origins of life's creative big-bang blast
Sent hurling through the dark unknown forever since;
Now as then the doorway to the soul's experience.
For the cosmic aspect only veils the task
Of the microcosmic world his thought must grasp.
This opposing force is inward too and what men see
Is not the stark objective picture of reality.
One world hides another one as quantum physics knows;
A more elusive concept than thinking minds suppose.
As great a puzzle as the outer world may be
The inner one is yet a greater mystery.
And hidden in the hubs of man's progressive wheels
Churns the deep anxiety his inner world conceals.

THE DARK PRINCE.

He now is in the process up to his chin.
Little though he knows, this new path will begin;
Beyond the present one surrounded by diversion
To lead him down before his secret self-aversion...

THE UNKNOWN WOMAN.

Though first he must pay for his sense of independence --
Its fantasy a blinding compensation --
As future tasks will soon demand attendance
Far exceeding any conscious explanation.
Everything his lonely heart has not achieved

Outweighs the little gods once pouring from his lips;

For his arrogance conceals a nature ill-conceived

And soon his heart will tremble as the measure tips

Weighed down by what his gods had not perceived.

Soon his heart will tremble at the fate he found;

His blinding arrogance turn upside-down.

The love he sought will pierce his soul like lightning.

What once was warm will soon be quick and frightening.

To love, did he think it was an easy thing:

A gently rocking crib of little birds to sing?

Did he not know it would tear his very being

This force enticing men to their own awakening?

He will love her with a pain he never knew before

And through it find himself before the bolted door

Of the spirit his own lust had locked within him;

Who grinned at him through every urgent lonely night.

How nearly crazy will a new desire send him

Down inside the darkness of his trembling heart's delight.

When his ecstasy subsides and he's alone in bed

This new desire will expose its midnight task;

And he will wonder how his trembling heart was led

So unwittingly before a world so dark and vast.

THE DARK PRINCE.

Unwitting though prepared by his own reality

For the blacker image trembling hearts can scarce relieve.

This gradual emergence of his personality

Is not a process culture knows or can conceive.

It draws him far indeed from a cultural sphere
Down before an inner world of guilt and pain and fear.

THE ODDLY SHAPED MAN.

I've spent half my life hiding from myself --
Searching through the landfill of convention --
Scavenging the world at best and little else
Pretending it was all my own invention.
I did the things most men are urged to do:
Got a job and married – had a child;
Though I marched along in step without a clue
That what I once revered was now reviled.
The tired traditions of the godly and devout
Long aggrieved my heart with uncertainty and doubt;
And slowly they developed through advancing years
To symbolize my own rejected fears.
They now pierce my heart only from within
Like serpent's venom through the man I thought I'd been.
I'd come to believe in a strange elusive circus
Too dazzled by it to extrapolate its dark intent;
Too enthralled with self-deceit to see the purpose
Of bothering my consciousness with what it meant.
With clowns and silly acts, jugglery and side-shows
I tried ardently to please the strangers in the rows.
I performed with all my might to make the crowd applaud
While in my dreams at night I saw the picture of a fraud.
Doubly I determined to exceed their expectation
Holding hands with shadows of the virtues I intended;
Bowing to the audience in my imagination

Amid the grand ovations of the image I pretended;
Clutching at the accolades this idol deigned to give
To any ego whose perverted sense of pride
Could fool itself anent the life it feigned to live --
And yet ignore the image of the soul inside.
I still imagined some new act could make it right;
That a greater effort yet would give the folks a show.
And as I watched my own performance I lost sight
Of the dreaming world opposing me below.
I was hypnotized indeed by the actor I created
Though secretly my role became a character I hated.
Yet what else could I do when the velvet curtain rose
But follow the direction of the script I chose?
Trying not to think about the dreams left unexplored
Whispering the secrets of the soul I'd long ignored.
Slowly its reality with each rehearsal
Forced upon my consciousness a dark reversal;
And the honesty I lacked to see behind the scene
Now resounds inside my mind with every play:
What can you be doing? What does all this mean?
How has such an image led you so astray?

THE DARK PRINCE.

The little man obsessed with his circus-like illusion
Will slowly yield before the depth of his confusion
And finally admit that his rejected dreams
Secretly reveal a life of two extremes:
One fancies him exempt from such a foolish game
While the other only revels in it just the same.

The fake laughter over-spilling from his too-wide mouth

Only masked the anguish when the matter turned about.

But as humbling as it is to pierce his vanity

He's still on the surface of this veiled humanity.

Far below the image now dissolving in his head

Lies the deeper darker one to which his soul is wed.

THE UNKNOWN WOMAN.

What is this shadow-image lurking in his soul

But a preordained demand to make him whole?

The secret in her bosom Nature holds so close

Is for men to fight the things they fear the most.

These contain the gifts for which a man must long --

The reason it's so difficult and feels so wrong:

A real fear grips a man when he must come to own

That his life has been projected by a dark unknown...

THE DARK PRINCE.

He seeks to bribe this dark unknown with sentimental verse;

As if his musings could describe to him its heavy curse!

The half-acknowledged shadow he indulges in his song

Will soon consume the little path he now skips along.

He projects his misery to keep this curse away;

To protect him from the specters his beliefs allay.

Such illusions are a cultural creation

Though the real task lies in his imagination.

Everybody hides it from himself every day.

Each must seek a refuge in his own clandestine way;

And he is now a victim of this underworldly task

Every process of creation enters in
From the oldest regions of the minds of men.
The symbols they produce are strange indeed –
Stranger still the mysteries to which they lead.

Exposing his subservience to its collective mask.

The force of character beneath his imitation

Has been the captive of an unseen limitation.

What his thought imagines as its own driving force

Has only drawn him down before a deep remorse.

Why else would he seek harbor through projected deeds

Save to flee the burden of his own rejected needs?

His models only knew one way, the inner way was closed

And self-protection only nursed the profile he then posed

To hide this other side lest he be thought unknown --

At first from others, later from himself alone.

His inner war remained within that hidden part

To fuel the self-disdain in his forbidden heart.

It descended down where no light yet existed

Down inside the darkness like a knotted ball it twisted.

He himself allowed it whether consciously or not

For his stark naked flight finds him now in this hard spot;

Not only had allowed it but become a party too

Through the double-faced illusion of his conscious view.

He'd buried his own treasure to become the fool

Of a world bowing only to its own collective rule;

Where long ago his hopes were turned to sorrow and fright

As dark intuitions stole upon him in the night.

It seemed turned around to him from early on

Yet every day the world convinced him he was wrong.

For him to find a place amid this faceless crowd

He surfacely embraced the gods to which they bowed.

They carried him along until he secretly rebelled

Though many years were gone before the secret he compelled

Could finally reveal itself to his charade

And force a new perspective on the world these men parade.

He then became a stranger in a game of hide-and-seek

Stealing round the corners of their lives to take a peek.

But disaffected monsters only proved in the beginning

That good faith and promise are the oldest forms of sinning.

Pastors ever somber acted out the roles they learned

Conjured dead words from corpses, never felt what they taught;

Playing to a captive house for love they hadn't earned

Caught by fear and weakness and confused by what they thought.

Their homes were not the palaces their hearts had hoped;

They resigned themselves to little through their teaching.

Their souls were greedy as for other souls they groped

Unaware of their exaggerated reaching.

Who still grieves the little boy who couldn't understand?

How does this reluctant little boy become a man?

Part of him remained a child, still hoping and excited

For corpses with a new life to yet be reunited.

But that was a foolish dream he soon must sacrifice:

That ever a corpse rotten and black could be breathed new life.

All the monsters grinned and postured and knew all about it --

Gave the notions loud lip-service in others' presence;

Though at home in bed at night he came to doubt it

And something in him cursed at his own acquiescence.

But his intuitions frightened him beneath the guise

And he shuddered secretly at thoughts they might be right

While stealthily his thinking sought a compromise

And openly he praised the dark men thought was light.

They shook hands and laughed and prayed for all their friends

And their souls contained temptations for the things they feared.

Garish acts of loving robbed them briefly of their sins --

Still they cried alone at night when grief appeared.

He knew they feared this image just as he did too

And like them his outer pose was too-high prized;

Yet the lost and empty inner life he also knew

Could in his heart no longer be disguised.

He was worn and weary, too confused to find his way

Where every path is littered with the silent pleas

Of a backward world in ordered disarray

Who worships fear and cultivates disease;

Spreading like a fire with every new diversion

Feeling hallowed discontent in every gaze;

Hoping fervently to keep its own perversion

Safely locked within the god to which it prays.

But these were half-inventions of his own mind:

Elusive dreams he hoped perverted gods could find

Crouched behind the silhouette of someone else's door

To mock him through the windows in the clothing he once wore.

He was uncertain and doubted much, this oddly shaped man;

Only through his failure was he made to understand:

The shadow-grief which sought relief was no one else's blame

For the anger in his once-red cheeks was guilt and shame.

He'd seen such things in others as the weaknesses they had;

Thought he could interpret for them what were good and bad.

He didn't know his little life was no less bound --

For the very things he cursed against he shared;

Didn't know the glaring contradictions he once found

Were the very ones in which he was ensnared.

The evangelism he once so despised

Was his own unconscious righteousness he prized

To convince himself the fault in others lay

For signing Nature's spirit-life away...

These ideas will form the pathway leading down

Inside the nature his own youthful dream implied.

Without such insights he would only wander round

In the maze of contradictions he identified.

An older snake than Eden's strikes him from within

Though its forked tongue is not projected onto Eve.

It consumes itself: a symbol to the world of men

That even their most sacred truths may yet deceive.

His Eve is not the guilty one depicted in the book

Just as the snake contains a different allusion.

A darker nature will require him to look

To older sources to uncover his confusion...

But Eves, snakes, and round black dots are not his concern --

His thinking's now perverted by the modern life he leads.

Only when this curtain has been lifted will he earn

The privilege of struggling with those deeper needs.

THE ANCIENT KING.

This snake of paradise reveals his older face

When the Deity and he assume their natural place...

Of course such noble strife may never be fulfilled –

Nor yet its restlessness be wholly stilled.

The restlessness this energy provokes

Conceals a higher form than it evokes.

No man's consciousness can stand alone

Against the rush of Nature's swarming might;
Yet he shall claim no object as his own
As naked he is hurled through night on night.
Teeming shadow-worlds fly fleetly on
Through Nature's black and unrelenting flight
Flashing brilliant through the vast and dark unknown
And ever onward rushing shrink from sight...
What form of worship leads a man where none has trod?
Was spirit only born with Adam's waking eyes?
How many ancient names had men acclaimed as God
Before a newer faith proclaimed them all as lies?
What else were men to worship in the origin of mind
But the matrix of a Nature which awakened Time?
And the very beast with which their humanness had dueled
To free the human part of them the beast had ruled?
Has any god released them from the ancient beast
Whose savage images belie their storied past?
Have they yet embraced a human face whose motives ceased
To be but urges of the beast that face has masked?
A chronicle indeed this world of gods and men;
As far as one may penetrate one finds it's always been.
Mere idols men once deified before their gods were one
But when the modern veil is stripped away it still is done.
A cozy nest men fashion with their modern lore;
Repose in god-likeness above the history they bore --
Though no forgiveness welcomes them when heavenward they gaze
But the dark and foreign aspect of their former praise.
Indeed the Holy Spirit has descended from the skies
Yet no triumphant savior do their pleas entreat.

Buried deep in Nature's mystery their future lies

And everywhere she weaves their fate beneath their feet.

The idols modern man reveres to compensate his myth

Are still protection from the beast his soul's entangled with;

Bowing to the saviors of sophisticated tools --

Too wise to be instructed now by superstitious fools.

Did not long ago a god bestow what men conceived

As an image of the only truth to be believed?

Is the god-like truth residing in the intellect

To save their children from the beast they would neglect?

A long travail awaits this man by this design

Just as consciousness grew upward in the human mind.

Yet this task shall send him in the opposite direction

To re-create the origins of self-rejection.

THE DARK PRINCE.

All the tribute men bestow upon the god of science

Slowly steals away the mystic treasure-world within.

Like precocious children who pretend to being giants

They compensate the inner world by being supermen.

But when they face the needs beneath their stark defiance

This world will find them little children once again...

This man too must now review the mask deluding him

To take responsibility for who he is today.

Perhaps he then can look within the world eluding him

And begin to see it in a new productive way.

But first he must confront the wants and needs that swarm

In all his child-like fantasies in undeveloped form.

Hidden in these symbols is the way to Nature's plan

For deep within the child lies the history of man.

But this is not an easy world to penetrate --

Other deities must be appeased to feel it.

And the causal thought his mind was taught to fabricate

Is not the kind of thinking to reveal it...

On The Symbolic Nature of the Inner World

The unconscious attracts the conscious mind to its aims via the symbol – at this stage the child, which signals future growth and development as well as the mythic connection with the unconscious experienced in childhood. Jung's empirical investigations show dream-symbols to be the means through which psychic energy is transferred to consciousness; the image is the form of that energy. Dreams often anticipate moods and feelings which may persist for a considerable time, allowing certain ideas in them to take hold and stimulate thought as it is slowly and subtly influenced toward a more symbolic reality.

He wanted to pretend he was an adult and so his adulthood was
fashioned out of childish perceptions of what an adult was
supposed to be. Thus it happened that his immature desires
eventually became impassioned within an adult body. The pretense
gradually became convincing because it had to be unless he was
to remain a child to himself; unless he was to stare starkly at
his own unconscious attempts to fit into his own natural place.
But such a process indeed is the forward goal of regression –
however ignorant of this fact he may be. For his adult actions
belie this childish image. Nature's child, however, can feel this.
He felt it when he was little. His inner world now gravitates
around such feelings. For, Nature's child is the offspring of
emotion and not developed nor sophisticated enough in the mind
of a rational adult to express itself in any other than a fantastic
manner. And his adulthood was never able to accede to this --
only the putative fact that a child is somehow less than an
adult because it is a child. But because it is Nature's child
it is also far beyond an adult; though his child-like fantasies

could never convince him. In this way adulthood is fooled when it looks at its children; fooled by its own exaggerated attempts to release itself from its own regressive nature. Being veiled in this manner adults feel their contradictoriness staring back at them through their children in whom contradictoriness is innocent and natural; yet in them it is a weakness and embarrassing and thus they embarrass their children. They embarrass and shame them into being children as if being a child were merely an inferior form of being human. But more, they embarrass themselves into their children and are then never quite able to retrieve themselves because that image is concerned with itself and Life, alone.

They reside there comfortably and securely, for Nature's child is too unformed and inadequate in their rational minds to convince them of things which their natures belie in them. Their self-consuming fantasies are then transferred into their little inadequate images of themselves which they even name after themselves as if a little inadequate image should be proud for being attached to a bigger more sophisticated inadequate image whose negative virtues have reappeared in itself. They teach their children to somehow be grateful for this confusion and they lord over all they have given and speak nothing of all they have taken. They grab at their child-likeness until it is all mangled and twisted and they spit its natural innocence back out at it as if it were a crime -- and their children the guilty parties who secretly conspire to rob them of their esteemed illusions of themselves. They make them suffer for this alleged transgression as surely as if they had confined mankind to a gaol; chained its self-respect in the darkness and spooned it just enough of the pabulum of self-knowledge to hide

its own beastly lack of development; diluted its spirit with upside-down
reflections cast outside itself like ugly reprehensible things
serving only to accumulate the embarrassment of being human and
needful and vulnerable. They make monsters of their children
who are not sophisticated enough to conceal their brutishness --
like they are; not sophisticated nor developed enough to be able
to relieve it upon others and so it remains buried in their own
emotions. At last, with the abetment of adult instruction their
children's inadequacies transform into vanities and begin to
metastasize over the years until such time as they must release
their monstrous emotional illusions onto another innocent
generation who can then proudly embrace their own heritage --
deeply in love with it -- all the while hating themselves for their
monstrous embarrassment, their vulnerable little inadequacies, their
lack of sophistication, and their innocent natures.

THE UNKNOWN WOMAN.

Finally his pretense was convinced it was adult;
For he was long ago compelled to seek this worldly cult
By perceptions of maturity his childhood fashioned then
From images his innocence absorbed from other men.
But something in him never seemed to fit quite right
With this image introjected by his childish sight.
Nonetheless he was convinced by his own innocence
Through fantasy to purchase this adult indifference.
His dreams were soon impassioned by a fanciful desire
To overcome the innocence such fantasies require;
Otherwise his childhood might encourage his regression
To a nature inconsistent with adult repression.

Though his childish mind could not evaluate it

A part was left behind to later re-create it;

For even his adult-ery could not extinguish

This child-like life the grown-up world cannot distinguish.

Nature's child is not developed in the outward mind

Enough to offer more than what his innocence defined;

Not enough for entrance to a world of grown-up men

Whose natures seek a refuge from the violence done to them

By the fantasies of others and the innocence once shred

In a world of men whose childhoods had been long since dead.

How could he have ever known in his mature mind:

Such a vital part of living would be left behind?

Only afterward to form the outer world's reflection

And offer back the mirror of his own self-rejection.

THE ANCIENT KING.

The once-compelling outer life he sought before

Shall further still dissolve within his concrete mind;

For this inner process yet requires more

Than the literal conceptions he shall leave behind.

The childish aspects of his personality

Are creative qualities his culture couldn't use;

And they now comprise the individuality

Buried deep within that child's collective views.

The little stream released when the lightning struck

Shall slowly be increased by his confusion

As his spinning wheels are only deeper stuck

And his soul begins to dwarf his old illusion.

The outer man shall fade and Nature's child grow great;

This movement's tension shall compel him to his fate.

New life shall be revealed through the needs he must atone;

He then shall suffer things he needs to feel to carry on.

The weight of children's dreams only men can stand to bear

And with that burden if he stands: a man becomes aware.

THE ODDLY SHAPED MAN.

If suddenly my thinking went from wrong to right

Would I make excuses for the little I possess?

Would I beg the darkness for the meagerness I fight

To circumscribe the feelings I must now confess?

I don't want a lot and I never really did --

But even that is more than thought can now discern.

For had it ever pierced inside the little needs I hid

My thinking would have never justified such small return.

What kind of thinking could excuse the bare desire

For the love I never had and never knew was there?

What would those dark thoughts within me then require

To satisfy the longing my own wants declare?

How does one beg the darkness? Who endeavors to excuse

Or even justify the begging of another's pleas?

His small desire then for another to abuse

The twisted needs of his own nature to appease.

Who else hears the wanting spilling out of me

But the shadow-image of the child I left behind?

For the begging and excusing are an empty plea

To the ghosts of love existing once within my mind.

How could I excuse myself from wanting anyway

Or overlook another's pleadings for the same things?

For no one knew the depth of guilt or where it lay
So we settled only for the pain such wanting brings.
Must we live with only guilty needs and never know
We saw each other longingly through strangers' eyes?
Stealing through the emptiness our hearts could never show
But through the anger meant to mask our lonely cries?
What about the false honor lodged inside my throat --
Like a stopper it chokes me but what does it mean?
Is it time's forgotten loss from feelings so remote
Our twisted begging only felt them as obscene?
Is this the flood of passion spilling out of me
Now upon this hostile make-believe reality?
Where you hurl your painful life at me and I at you
For buried needs we were convinced could not be true?
And deep inside each other's guilt the needs we stole
Flooded out through tongue and fist and twisted soul.
But glaring eyes and gritted teeth and gnarled face
Cannot convince me even in this lonely place;
Though I must confess: it frightened me back then
For all the guilty wants and needs it trapped within.
But who then had enough respect for his own pain
To try to feel it there within that dark domain?
So we all just walked away and said goodbye
Like nothing ever happened and we couldn't even cry
But for ourselves when we at last were left alone
With nothing but the painful guilt from needs unknown...
Jesus didn't die, he's still hanging from the cross;
Neither was he born again, he still is being stoned --
Even by the children who have suffered from our loss

For all the lonely guilt and pain left unatoned.

Spare the rod and spoil the child for he must suffer too

From the love inflicted on him by such buried pain

As causes needy souls to do the things they do

For all the wanting in their loving self-disdain.

So the children cried too for all their wants and needs;

Only later to defend themselves like mom and dad

Against each other and their natures and their own deeds

For the unaccepted wants and needs their natures had.

THE UNKNOWN WOMAN.

Want, need, and guilt are all one thing in the mind

Of a consciousness betrayed by Adam's missing rib:

This partial glow whose little flame so undefined

Must nightly yield to bedtime stories in its crib.

Only then is it diffused from its restricted sphere

As his dreaming mind continues unabated

Beyond this little glow inside the dark to peer

At the unexamined life his pride created.

This crying child reveals his own forgotten essence

Fastened to the only image conscious thought can see;

So enamored of itself and its candescence

Anything beyond it fades into obscurity.

Though what it sees in fantasies of self-enhancement

Must soon give up its wants for more important things:

The magical illusion of his self-enchantment

Has deceived too long the image of his sufferings.

The blind spots and guilty longing of such self-deceit

Will double-back the little world of his conceit.

His dark genuflection to his own behavior

Will then create an even stranger darker savior.

Though in his partial sight a demon now appears

He will see the need for it as his confusion clears.

For this is why his wants and needs are so confused --

Why his thought's desire by his guilt is so abused:

All the secret feelings his performance put aside

Are stealing back upon him through the dark divide.

And the deeds he parades before his wide-eyed child

With his own youth in some way must be reconciled.

The older patterns he once swore to overcome

Lay in deeper waters than his little wants can plumb.

Until his guilt reveals the depth of these emotions

His puddles of desire will appear as deep devotions.

At his present feeling-level he cannot be sure

Whether his own childhood was but fantasy's allure:

He was content in his small way but still confused

By the intuitions memory has since accused

Of infidelity to his own nature's needs

As in his innocence he processed others' deeds.

The screaming insults of the models he knew then --

Were they only the distorted souls of other men?

Even when they didn't scream, their anger seethed below

For reasons he accepted but could never know.

Secretly his soul retreated and he fled them

Though in his flight the more they were entwined in him.

Only now are they returning in this midnight task

To pose the questions innocence could never ask:

What force compelled him to the wants he thought he needed?

Which needs responded to the wants his guilt exceeded?

This emotional confusion is the conflict life reserves

For Nature's wisdom to impart the purposes she serves.

This future goal, however, is a scroll of seven seals

Until he owns the holy guilt his memory reveals.

THE DARK PRINCE.

This subtle movement parallels his own child's growth

For their unconscious destinies are intertwined;

And each reflects the growing nature of them both

On polar levels only in the conscious mind.

On the surface they're completely disconnected –

Underneath it they can scarcely be discerned.

It's on this deeper level Nature re-connected

The growing urge with which this man's concerned;

For, all the childhood fantasies he once projected

Are staring back at him through what his child has learned...

The symbols of this process feature life at every stage

Of Nature's dark transitions through maturity.

Their clothing changes only slowly with advancing age

And a man's self-awareness of his ambiguity.

For this objective world does not discriminate

The double-nature of the symbols he confronts.

Past and future co-exist in this unconscious state

As the man he'll be and the child he was at once.

THE ODDLY SHAPED MAN.

What would I give my child to guide her through the storms

Of her own childhood memories beguiled by surface forms?

Would I give her all the pain -- the hard enduring pain --
Our history bestowed us in its long proud tradition?
With complacent certainties our culture must maintain
To hide our beastly nature from our conscious recognition?
Would I reinforce this proud display of what her life should be
And deny the ugly aspects of my own humanity?
Stage a small performance with excruciating poses
In foolish pride so satisfied with what I preached?
All the while in stealthy secret symbiosis
To turn her from the future life for which she reached?
Self-righteous and correcting in my grand paternal role;
Unaware of, unreflecting on the damage to her soul?
Would I heap my petty fears upon her innocence
Only to condition her to what my love requires?
Pretending it is I and all the wisdom I dispense
Who reveals the only truth amid a world of liars?
What does any child need but sound adult advice
And wise instructive words to cloud her vision?
To blind her to the facts of daddy's vice
Which makes mistakes with every sure decision:
Choices governed by the childish fantasies I sought
To relieve me of the past I have rejected
In my flighty fit of rationalistic thought
To convince myself my child could be protected
From the ugly rage my own tradition taught.

THE DARK PRINCE.

The process now begins to pull him further down --
Below the consciousness of who he thinks he is --

Before an aspect of his life much more profound

Than his little needs to justify appearances;

Down before a distant land where images exist

Where reality is as reality does:

The world of fantasy his manhood has dismissed –

One where he must work to be the child he always was.

THE UNKNOWN WOMAN.

In his own youth anger was a proud emotion;

Others cowered at this power making men feel strong.

And it seemed relentless as does all compulsion

When the form of its activity is wrong.

It separated peoples' lives and like a thief

Only robbed them of the needs beneath their grief.

He tried to hide the anger raging in his ears

Though the twisted faces never ceased in all his years.

He hated all those faces and the pain they spread;

All the same their image pulsed beneath the life he led.

He was painfully compelled to have to fight it

But always in the world and never in his own heart.

As his sensitivity was tucked away inside it

The projection of his pain became a self-indulgent art.

He grew older and in angry ways he couldn't understand

Through fists exploded all the grief his heart had long repressed.

Hurting like the others he did crazy things he never planned

Never knew this grief was there until it pounded in his chest.

He spilled his seething anger out soiling those around him

With the same distorted model that rejects its own pain.

Of course its regularity continued to astound him

For without reflection who can see his own self-disdain?

His life was driven by the foolish pride of his deceit

And the self-destruction of the rage he justified --

Until his daughter laid his childhood at his feet

Through the world of feeling his own manhood had denied.

He soon could not explain away his guilty grief

By fighting others in projected self-defense;

Though in his wretchedness he managed some relief

In the dark retreat he forged to nurse his pretense.

This life has left a grievous mark upon his soul

A wound his consciousness may never fully yield;

But it leaves too the greater story to be told

Of the self-inflicted wound that must be healed.

For his toughness was his only self-protection;

Without it he would be the prey of other men

Who sought to steal away the precious self-perception

Only masquerading for the darker task within.

But when this process closed him to his former view

Those thieves revealed the image of his own devotions

To the cardboard musketeer his thought was pasted to

By the sweat and blood of his ignored emotions.

His secret fears collected in the image he portrayed

To become this greater conflict he so tried to hide.

And from the anger in the balled-up fists he once displayed

Emerged an image he no longer could abide.

No more could he abide it –

But in fact what concept has he of himself

To fight his way inside it?

An Objective Evaluation

Dreams impress upon consciousness its split from the deeper world of the repressed opposite, as it is increasingly drawn into the orbit of unconscious emotional demands. These compensations are relative to the individual but are also applicable in a general way to the extent that we are conditioned by the spirit of the times in which we live. The unique combination of inherited personal qualities dictates more the intensity with which certain functions such as feeling and thinking may compel attention. This is an objective conflict which heralds the changing spiritual orientation beginning to surface beneath ego-awareness: the underlying design of individuation to balance conscious functions – the urge to wholeness.

He was only partially constructed, being composed largely of upper parts. His arms and hands were rangy and constituted his only real physical motion. His voice compensated his lack of lower stability and was comprised of an inner silent fragment roughly akin to thinking -- though less the function of awareness than of automatic reaction -- and an audible fragment that while outwardly directed was acted upon by and only reacted to the disaffected nature of the inner dictates. The outer voice was brusque and demanding and projected the slender veneer of authority in his attempts to control the environment; but it was in reality only a compensation for his lack of control and the plaintive supplicative nature of his relation to his inner processes -- these being neither willed nor conscious.

He could not walk upright nor balance himself and this confined him to the floor where he tried to obscure himself by the furnishings except at such times as he felt compcllcd to ply certain demands upon certain sympathetic ears having chanced to be in the vicinity. Even then he remained mostly hidden by an object in the room, shouting and waving his arms so as to be only partially visible to create the illusion of being a whole person. Sometimes this was effective in manipulating whomever happened to be in the room -- though the most effective aspect of his pretense was the pity and repugnance his appearance elicited if ever he was glimpsed in his partial entirety.

There was, however, an invisible part of him -- perceived only by him and even then at very rare and unpredictable instances -- which bore a deeper image of his wholeness. At such unusual moments the outer voice was quiescent, and if it was reactive at all it reacted to the peace of solitude gravitating around this faraway magical image. Of course he had vague suspicions at such unusual moments that perhaps one or two of those with whom he had a symbiotic relationship -- the chance bystanders -- could somehow feel the presence of this image within an image and that the dim intuition of it rather than his transparent manipulations was what moved them to succumb to his demands. Furthermore, it was this strange convoluted double-image also preponderating even over their pity for him and their intense sorrow for his truncated condition. But in the end he always dismissed these vague suspicions, for they would only lead him to the self-examination he worked so hard to avoid.

Actually, in his small way he did work very hard at training himself to be effective but as he had not the tools to create at will the appearance of the magical image and its wondrous effects, his training and work remained stuck on the superficial level of demand and manipulation; for he had not the slightest idea how to steer his efforts toward promoting the efficacy of these magical feelings.

What he also did not understand was that this image and its fleeting emotions -- though unseen and rarely felt -- were always present; otherwise the persons upon whom they effected a relation to him would surely have remained unaffected, for the consciousness of their appearance was so seldom that if their presence were confined only to those moments it would have been impossible to obtain to a lasting effect -- even on himself -- much less on those whom he attempted to manipulate.

It was only in these rare and singular moments of their appearance when any real learning or appreciation of the subtler movements of his life took place. The rest of his hours were as if suspended in a fourth-dimensional existence which moved forward in Time much like any other life but it was a life in which nothing of any substantial value was added to it or enacted by it and it enhanced nothing and was enhanced by nothing. This suspended world and the unconscious feelings evoked by it were at the core so frightening he could not confess to their existence, leaving the greater share of his available energy to exhaust itself in the processes of reactive compensation and manipulation which so thoroughly characterized his being-in-the-world. The intense emotional release he would undoubtedly experience upon the admission of this suspended passage through Time he considered his life would have gone far in creating a fertile bed for the growth of his lower functions; but his urge to reflection creativity and imagination had been stunted by his thinking and his existential sedation.

As a result of the compensations dictated by his dependence on manipulation, his dissociated amusements consisted primarily of the misfortune of others and only the coarse and ridiculous nature of accidental mishap could provoke his laughter. Indeed, his laughter was little more than an exaggerated sneer and behind the sounds of it lay emotions laden with sadness, hostility, and fear. The only meager satisfaction he experienced was the selfish and infantile fulfillment of expectation resulting from external compliance with his demands and the brief self-gloating which lifted his otherwise heavy depressing life of rolling around on the floor from this piece of furniture to that in an effort to conceal his pain and embarrassment from himself and others. It was difficult to speak of humanness when referring to him, for he was so incomplete the euphemism seemed hardly to apply. Nor was the epithet "animal" applicable; for, his habitual reliance upon manipulation, his total immersion in reactive compensation, and his abject sense of humor seemed fitted only for some in-between world of fragmented hodge-podge which defied any real classification -- a modern missing link. Indeed, his lower functions were so twisted and perverted from lack of use, their atrophy had severely conditioned the neural pathways of his thinking; though because of his inability to recognize or admit this perverted lower world, the state of his reasoning powers seemed to him through his illusion not only unaffected but even normal and healthy. His refusal to examine this degrading form of existence caught him ever faster in his convoluted preoccupations and compelled him ever further toward his singly focused activities. He was unable to relax this focus for the inner tension and anxiety pushing him into the unconscious cycle of attraction and repulsion defining him. The compensating fantasies resulting from these extreme states were so hostile to his self-image they precluded him from observing himself almost completely.

He was exhausted most of the time from extraneous activity; his off-balance flailing being a sore attempt to regain moral equilibrium, for his upper extremities alone could not possibly provide support through his upside-down development. This grave condition could not practically be compensated without it being completely obvious to any outside party of the nature of the compensations. In fact, had he intuited any notion of the peculiar picture he presented to others it would have wounded him so severely as to impede him from obtaining what scant emotional sustenance as he was able and thrown him back on himself so powerfully he could scarcely have endured it. These compensations presupposed an objective basis for his personality and its expressions and this described the conflict between the furtive concealment consuming the bulk of his hours and the unobserved Nature-given image intended to mediate his opposed instinctual functions.

The form of the compensations was determined by the peculiar character of accidental circumstance: his own idiosyncratic reactions based on his own individual inadequacies and insecurities developed as a response to the environment -- and as a response to the gulf between these developed reactions and the urgings of the magical image. However, the line between the demands of the environment and the inner urgings of the natural image was blurred to indistinction. As a result, the whole of his complaints, dissatisfactions, and preconceived conflicts were lodged very concretely in the outside world and formed the movie screen onto which were projected his emotional impediments and obstacles. In fact, the chance bystanders moving in and out of his life, being whole in their physical appearance, came to represent this holographic image of wholeness and he resented that image through those persons for the impossible demands it orchestrated backstage of the performance acted out by his compensations.

THE UNKNOWN WOMAN.

So where amid this hodge-podge does his soul reside:
The magic image his frenetic efforts hide?
He must find a way to penetrate this inner guise
And generate the function it was meant to realize.
It mediates the images flowing through perception
Immediately inward to a process of reflection;
Crowning Nature's premium for conscious recognition
Of the inner aspects of her own core condition.

THE ANCIENT KING.

There was a time when modern science first began
That seekers sought to weigh the soul of man.
They weighed a man at his last breath
Pronounced him dead and after death
They checked the scale by which to see
Whatever mass their instruments might free.
A man can scarcely measure what his soul weighs
Though he knows it can be heavy and direct;
As if its gravity had somehow worked its ways
On the weightless objects his imaginings project.
At other times too it seems so very light
A man feels heaven's angels had possessed him;
As if he'd sprouted wings and were capable of flight

Despite the former gravity that once depressed him.

It seems the instruments so long ago employed

Were not quite fitted for this subtle task;

And still today this enigmatic void

Defies direct perception through the conscious mask.

How can science grasp it through objective norm?

How does ego penetrate its own subjective form?

Experience and observation are the base of science --

Cannot a man's emotions yield to its appliance?

The precision of the measurements depends

On the instruments by which he apprehends.

His subjective thinking and its insufficience

Cannot theorize a concept of the whole.

For this a man must turn to the unconscious

To yield objective data of the soul.

Feeling is described, weighed, and evaluated

According to the values of the source innate

In the scales of measure Nature's core created

To bind his lower functions to his inner fate.

When subjective consciousness connects to this

Through the compensating image it expresses

It can almost be objective nonetheless

If it restricts itself to what the soul confesses...

Such ideas do not produce immediate reward

And certainty is not among their list of fruits.

Only those whose natures are in ill-accord

Shall be driven to such difficult pursuits.

The study of matter is welcome relief

To the concrete urge for fixed explanation;

For learning of the soul shall lead a man to grief:

Such is the essence of the Christian compensation.

Yet the soul is one thing and the spirit quite another;

Both contain possessive qualities that veil the other.

Their alluring fantasies throughout the world have spread;

He must search his soul to bring them back inside his head.

This spirit-process too is an act of creation

Every bit as tangible as that of science.

Where would mankind be without imagination

To form an inner image of the soul's experience?

THE DARK PRINCE.

The spirit has possessed him in his rationalistic air

For the intellect cannot detect a spirit anywhere.

Yet it functions in him just as sure as he's a man

Though he laughs at notions of a hidden spirit-land.

It slumbers deep within the outer images he sees --

A heavy load to shoulder for a thinking mind's demand

To give up foolish notions of the ancient mysteries

Once relating men to gods they fought to understand;

Whose very lives were formed around their efforts to appease

The motive force behind the fate of every living man.

He fancies he knows all about the urgings of his fate

Though he grieves beneath the images they now create.

They weave the garment of the ancient spirit's cloak

So heavy for his modern legs he shakes beneath its yoke.

He and every other Atlas struggling to stand

Thrust before this modern quandary without a god;

Science-driven creatures reinventing Nature's plan

Divining paths upon a fairytale facade;

Flying on the magic carpet of unconscious dreams

Bracing for catastrophe and living life in minutes

Ignoring all the consequence of their diverted schemes

To build amusement parks around their old religious tenets...

And he, projecting his minutiae onto sacred ground

Seeing priceless gems in all the pebbles he has found:

Where every vein of thought contains a streak of gold --

The story of his life becomes a mighty venture told;

But every mountain's hidden peak reveals the sad disgrace

Of the little foothills his imaginings embrace.

How fanciful to criticize the lack of others' sight

As he blindly bobs around his modern carousel!

His own soul obscured by the symptomatic flight

Through the same diversions such unconscious dreams compel.

Can he conceive these fantasies of self-division

Which unacknowledged myth divines his little course?

Which hidden fate anticipates with each decision

Its plan to draw him down before his nature's source?

His life was once determined by the fate of other men

Until his soul decided it was too collective.

Now he is afflicted with another form of sin

As the serpent weaves around the fruit of its objective:

To strip the classic cloth of Christian self-deception

Sewn within the modern fig leaf of statistics;

Still suffering forgotten gods and their inception

Of a space-age spectacle no intellect can fix...

But many knots both large and small must be untied

Before he meets the gods of his collective deeds.

If honestly he listens to the voice inside
And follows Time whichever way it leads
The ebb and flow of its relentless tide
Will slowly surface everything he needs.

THE ODDLY SHAPED MAN.

I must be quite contentious and accustomed to strife --
Aloof and pretentious in my solitary life;
Comforted by sarcasm, admiring my wit
Loathe to reveal myself and even proud of it;
Above the world on a pedestal of self-abuse
For the fancied inner nature of a half-recluse.
I sensed for years it was a deeply troubled state
But only my condolence had need for the past;
And I blamed a hostile world for my ignoble fate
Imagining my thought as its iconoclast.
I scarce considered I could travel back in time
Without being caught in my own science-fiction;
Never knew the living past concealed within my mind
Was trapped there by the myth of my conviction.
The Rip Van Winkle of my own fairytale
Has awakened from a dream forever gone
And lonely strangers now appear behind the veil
Of the forty years of fantasy I slept upon.
In their eyes how strange I seem and out of place
From too long sleeping with my self-contention;
As the wrinkled hopes of by-gone years upon my face
Reveal the furrows of their unforeseen dimension.
Where am I? What am I? Whose plans were swept astray?

Where's the young man I once fancied in the mirror?

Vaguely in a distant world he slowly crept away

And forty years more dreaming couldn't bring him nearer.

Yet still I see his shadow in this older man's face --

A parody of faded dreams I can't embrace --

Returning my condolences grown twice their size

Than when I once consigned them to the past's disguise.

This elusive crowd of strangers I projected

For the youthful musketeer I once protected

Is swirling round me through the fog of my pretension:

A frightening inversion of my past invention.

Now through my confusion I can see their salty faces

Crying out for meaning from those forty years before;

Though in their anguish I can see the lonely traces

Of the younger man whose fantasies they bore.

Did the past awaken or a future come to me?

Are these reflections of the me who was?

Or only odd projections of a world to be

So strangely ordered by the things time does?

THE DARK PRINCE.

He did go back in Time though his future to reveal --

For his intellect a crazy contradiction.

But the curve of inner space is far more real

Than any surface paradox of science-fiction.

Beneath its stark projections lies a greater aim indeed

Than the fiction of his consciousness can see;

One objective science must eventually concede

Lies far beyond the scope of rationality...

The Real Contradiction Begins to Emerge

A changing consciousness begins to sense the gravity of its own historical foundations, causing a profound collision between the two perspectives. The conflict of opposites now moves into the foreground as ego intuits the deeper pull of functions which exceed choice and free will. In terms of Jung's energic theory, this is one of the vital steps toward a conscious recognition of the inner gradient -- the narrow gate referred to in the Bible. The reactions that follow reflect the fear of being taken over by the "alien will" of the unconscious and its steady aim toward wholeness. As it continues to seize hold, dreams flow along this gradient to establish bridges which would further connect an isolated modern perspective to the still-living history of the instinctual psyche.

Hidden in the human brain beyond the microscope
(Notwithstanding men's amusement at such propositions)
Inherent in the cells where Nature's darkest urges grope
(Beyond the worship of objective suppositions)
Mythic creatures gather in the gaps of consciousness
(Such fantasies are soon denied and denigrated)
Deep within the intellect's inherent pompousness
(The secret force behind the life it imitated.)
The creatures forming in the shadows of the dark unknown
(Who reveal the opposites of earthly contradiction)
Force a man to flee the facts his life is based upon
(A different and stranger form of science-fiction.)
For the base of thought is more than philosophical
(This weird inheritance from early generations.)
Its roots strike even down to the botanical
(As vine-like shapes anticipate all thought's formations)

Where Nature's living symbols grow like leaves on trees

(Quite removed from scientific declarations)

Cast aside to seek their own release as they may please

(Only later to appear as compensations.)

Their only chance a conscious mind to penetrate

(Despite their dark intrusions into every act)

Is when consciousness itself is in diminished state

(The unadorned expression of its earthly fact.)

It is here the ancient and the modern are combined

(Older themes belie the most contemporary dress.)

And strange are these intrusions in the sleeping mind

(But just as real as any science nonetheless.)

THE DARK PRINCE.

Strange indeed to see his youth through the lens of older years;

The shame of his unconsciousness creates a haunting veil.

It undermines his god-likeness and forms his greatest fears

And it drags along behind him like a saurian tail

Stirring up the mythic dust of ancient culture's tread

In the wars with fantasies it then considered real;

Plunging this man's mind before the images he fled

For the purpose of emotions too confused to feel.

All the fancy knowledge of his causal education

Comprises his evasion from this dark reality --

In Time decayed to form the veil of self-negation

Designed to barter off his personality.

As much as he would push such insights far away

Not much longer will his modern flight persist;

Hidden far below the mask his thinking will betray

Lives the foreign world in which his mythic lords exist.

This cave is dark and deep and far away from thinking:

One where feelings creep in Time's forgotten mystery;

And in its depths his consciousness is slowly sinking

To prepare a journey into ancient history...

But he must linger further with the personal regrets

Of the smaller life responsible for his demise

Before he can determine what these ancient silhouettes

Conceal beneath the fluid forms of their disguise.

THE ODDLY SHAPED MAN.

Have two worlds arisen where there once was one?

Colliding in the depth of my imagination?

Just when I dreamed the new life I discovered

By the power of my thinking was uncovered

A new image of the pain I thought I once endured

Flickers in the twilit realm my thought obscured.

THE UNKNOWN WOMAN.

This stark pain behind the intellect's retreat

Is a dark domain and a force he cannot cheat.

This task has been conceived as a fraudulent deed

By the credulous mask of his rational creed;

Yet suffering remains despite his fancied will

For these growing pains are now becoming all too real.

How does he respond when he objectifies his pain:

Creates its dark reactions in another's soul?

Is confronted through his loving with his self-disdain

And must admit he suffers in his own black hole?

This ancient cave has always been a sacred place;
It represents the older regions of the mind.
And split-off aspects in him will be forced to face
This dark retreat by which the Spirit is divined.

Does he consider then his self-rejection too
Or does he blame the other for his discontent?
Such is the childishness of his subjective view:
That pain on either plane could make a man repent.
How can he repent for things he doesn't understand?
Though blame and fault dement the life of each and every man
The notion of repentance on humility relies
As well as on a higher force a man can recognize.
And his humility is hidden in a false ideal
For the god of thought cannot instruct a man on how to feel.
He bounces back and forth between more basic deities:
The jealous gods of love and fear and thought's velleities.
He must hide them often for they never let him rest;
They may overpower consciousness at any time.
When they do he feels their burden like a man possessed
Though not until the flood abates can he perceive the crime.
How does one repent the very crime of ignorance
Except he first acknowledge what he can't control?
Set his sights upon the task of the experience
Of repressed emotions lying hidden in his soul?
His fraud is taking refuge in his lonely cave
For any refuge soon becomes a prison.
His fraud is thinking the excuses he once gave
Could ever justify this strange new world arisen.
His ideal image is as false as any claim
Of a thinking flown beyond the world from which it came.
His dark world is what he'll be as well as what he was;
How he may relate to both depends on what he does.

He has compassion in his frantic heart, I know --

But what does it accomplish? Where does it go?

This shadow-task was set before him long ago

Heavy in the lonely conflicts he espoused

Waiting for his fancied consciousness to grow

And birth the nature this predicament aroused.

His awareness of this world has only just begun;

The core of all his lonely sufferings is here.

But Time no more affords for him the luxury to run --

He must confront the symbols of his soul as they appear.

THE DARK PRINCE.

A world of darkness on him eerily descended

The knotted ball his self-indulgence long repressed;

Formed from images his thought left unattended

The life beneath the anger it has since expressed.

He thought: with effort he could make it disappear

The very strategy provoking this unholy sphere.

It pulled his vision downward by the gravity of mass

To re-acquaint him with an unintended past.

In his old conception things grew grand and tall

To represent the wishful nature of his sight;

But down and wide and deep inside grew this black ball

And only in the dark can he discern its light.

The upward angle of his childish narrow eyes

Could not judge properly an object's shape or size;

Only feel the weight and the alien sensation

Of a living force relating to its own creation.

When his lofty thought was brought beneath this heavy weight

The fantasies once bearing him upon his flight
Sailed up in the clouds like clouds to dissipate
And a dark unyielding universe eclipsed the light.
His fragmentary consciousness was paralyzed;
His old desires half-revered and half-despised.
The spirit's black dot lying dormant in his youth
Pulled him down before the darkness of its own truth.
His nights could not protect him from the tasks of day
Nor could the day relieve him of the night's demand;
His thought no longer able to explain away
The strange emotions of a life he never planned.
In his ego's panic at this natural descent
The self-anointed mask of consciousness was rent
To manifest a world beyond imagination --
Indeed the very fountainhead of its creation:
The abyss of life where only images reside;
The enigmatic void from whence this black ball grew.
It will expose the magic trick of his objective side
To turn his thinking round his own subjective view...
But there is ever more for him to contemplate
Before he gains a knowledge of this heavy weight.
As dark and painful as the process seems right now
Before still darker gods will be he forced to bow.
His attitude will soon be readjusted
As he becomes acquainted with his own black hole;
And the surface images for which he lusted
Are broken down and processed in his soul.

THE ODDLY SHAPED MAN.

How many phantoms has my thinking now dissected?

And each endeavor by my nature yet rejected?

It seems like thousands in my lone confusion

Doubled in the mirror of my own illusion;

My object of pursuit unseen but darkly felt

Slowly overtaking me inside myself.

My head is crowded, night and day are one;

I search in vain the reasons for the things I've done.

The lion's courage in my heart I thought was real

Is now the frightened victim of the pain I feel.

A dark entanglement surrounds the steps I take;

I stumble through the maze of each new choice I make.

Emotions once repressed have broken through their guise;

Faces once familiar I no longer recognize.

The flow of time is now peculiarly disordered

As if reality with dreams were sliced and quartered.

A strange force has turned around the world I used to know;

Right is wrong, the sun is gone, the stars are down below.

The mannequin of yesterday lies far behind me:

The tattered remnants of a man who once defined me.

Naked and alone I stand stripped of his protection

Exposed to darkness crowding in from each direction.

The shattered pieces of my life exist no more

Faded in the dusk of what my scattered life is for.

The need I feel for old ideals cannot sustain that life;

The love I now embrace calls forth only pain and strife.

My grief only magnifies as each tear burns my cheek

But the tears do not provide me the relief I seek.

My head circles wildly as I strain with all my might;

All around me lay the pieces of the ghosts I fight.

I've forced apart the gates of my own humanity

Staggered weary to the furthest reach of sanity;

My own heart I've writhed and cried and suffered inside out --

Yet unappeased still labor on uncertainty and doubt.

THE DARK PRINCE.

Hemmed in by God on all sides like Job he struggles;

And his pursuit means other things pursue him too.

Relentlessly the feeling-world his thinking juggles

Brings him closer to the conflict of his conscious view.

The torment thrust upon him from this dark abyss

Is Nature's dispatch to a partial consciousness:

She strives now to inform him of *her* wants and needs

And give him strength to follow on the path she leads.

How a man must carry on when he is forced to see

That the life he once conceived is not Reality!

He may feel his little world is being torn apart

But in fact it's being put together quite unseen;

And he's further than he knows from the inside of his heart

Or his notions of insanity and what they mean.

THE UNKNOWN WOMAN.

He's not the victim of an angry god's invective

Sending wrathful thunderbolts of punishment and pain.

He must remind himself the process is objective;

To think outside his merely personal domain.

But how else can his trembling thought be made to see:

His life is subject to a fate he can't control?

That beneath his thinking is a greater force than he

Seeking to reveal to him the nature of his soul?

This obscure moral process must depend on more

Than simply choosing to obey a god's command.

Which god will he obey? Which one will he implore?

When two crossed gods of equal strength before him stand?

One is right the other wrong according to his view:

The great deception of the life he knew before;

Yet however he perceives it there is little he can do

For his former life is gone and Nature's closed that door.

The one she opens now brings the opposites to light

Unveiling secret truths beyond his preconception

To temper with a new sight the views of wrong and right

Which form the basis of his modern self-perception.

It will expose the partial attitude of consciousness

Flitting round its fantasies in airy self-pursuit

In the highest branches of the tree of righteousness

Thinking it had planted all the seeds of Love and Truth --

Though half-acknowledged grew to be a thing of wretchedness

And in the end bore little more than ignorance as fruit.

THE DARK PRINCE.

The cheap facade he financed with the treasure in his soul

Is quickly running out of credit with the man below.

The life he once invested in is out of his control

For the loan's conditions call for more than he could know.

The debt accruing from his youthful self-deception

Must be fully rendered from the life he leaves behind

Until it is depleted of his half-perception
And he accepts the humble place his misery assigned.
This task has led him down inside the knotted sphere
Concealing images his thinking long repressed.
How he perceives the inner man is hidden here
Whose image only surfaces when he's depressed.
But repression and depression are in fact related
To form the tension aiming at a new direction.
He must fight them both for how his thinking has created
This upside-down collision with his own reflection...

Mental Health as a Social Concept

The conflict of opposites deeply affects consciousness as it begins to withdraw its projections from the external world and accept its struggle internally, fostering the recognition of a higher spiritual authority. The more frightening, rejected aspects of the personality then begin to impress themselves as living values with a vital meaning for the individual. The fear and anxiety of losing control is tempered by reflection. Jung once wrote that no one who ever had any wits is in danger of losing them in this process; however, there are many who never knew until then what their wits were for.

THE ANCIENT KING.

    The concept of one's mental health is relative indeed;

    Primarily a social one for cultures to assess

    The useful products of the citizens they breed

    To work within the sanction of the values they profess.

    But a culture has no conscious point of reference:

    No place outside itself to judge its valuations;

    Its health or sickness no criterion for deference

    To its own psychology or that of other nations.

    Every man appears to suffer likewise from this fate

    Though facts do not support this from a natural perspective:

    The psyche functions in a way itself to regulate

    And beyond his preconceptions lives its own corrective.

    By this redemptive course the opposites cooperate.

    When they do the process functions in a Normal way;

    But conscious values have a tendency to deviate --

    To shake the bonds when culture holds too strong a sway

In a man whose inner nature has been drawn by fate

To the undiscovered path his sufferings betray.

The more opposed the more this law then compensates;

The more it compensates the more his fate to stray

Until finally the open conflicts it creates

Reveals the Nature in a man of mortal clay.

Culture too is driven by the same mechanism

And when its values steal astray it too must pay

With war and gore and every human cataclysm

Since first began the fate of man in Abel's day.

This fight between the conscious mind and Nature's will --

A war this man's unconscious plan has long prepared --

Has been battled to the point of a real stand-still

And a split decision now has been declared.

This grueling test though consciousness shall never win

For his enemy is not the one within his sights.

He shall soon discover from the battle he's been in:

It is a greater *inner* power he now fights.

This power is the only judge for such a man

Driven by his misery to seek beyond the sphere

Of the confines of collective culture's happy plan

To tell him what his life is for and why he's here.

Its concepts of the sane and normal are conditioned

By values from a source exceedingly remote;

So obscure in its reaches men have long petitioned

The only notions their confusion could promote:

Is it a god? Collective fate? Is it objective?

This power bidding men to do the things they do?

Or only products of a thinking so subjective

It had no other concepts to ascribe it to?

It is a sore affliction men must struggle with

To never know the object of their own devotions;

But this compels the spirit to create a myth

To formulate the meaning of its *own* emotions.

If a man discovers he's in conflict with it

Soon enough his nature shall reveal its dark design;

But in a form at first perceived as epithet

To compensate the concepts he could not define.

THE ODDLY SHAPED MAN.

I'm sick. This is the epithet I've used to characterize
myself: the one I've internalized from the traditional structure I was
embedded in -- that I'm so dissatisfied with; the same I have leaned
on and depended on to support me which support consists of
making me feel sick...

THE UNKNOWN WOMAN.

Everywhere its mocking voice cries out a muted curse:

Are the values we made sacred in your heart grown cold?

Now think you from the breast of Higher Wisdom nurse?

In your small hand the coin of Greater Truth would hold?

Imagine our reality you would reverse

For no more than the twisted tale your life has told?

How could such a little man in a world so great

Fancy he could redefine what only gods create?

THE ODDLY SHAPED MAN.

This bowl of my personality into which has been poured
this traditional structure of support is itself no longer able to
contain such things. The off-stream of rejected material
incapable of being fitted into this made-for-the-mass bowl is in
fact my individuality; the individuality siphoned off and
rejected in favor of the cherished identification with my perceived
sickness...

THE UNKNOWN WOMAN.

The hidden self cries out as well from the dark unknown;
Its haunting pleas unable too to be appeased:
First you rise to lofty height and then sink like a stone;
One day are agonized another day are pleased --
All for a strange reality you thought your own
Yet by a dark fantastic opposite is seized.

THE ODDLY SHAPED MAN.

I'm sick. I came to believe this of myself because I accepted the
unreflected past of a mouthpiece-of-the-mass requiring the
epithet of sickness to conceive a concept of difference.
Acceptance of this difference on any level was the very
definition of sickness for this mass-minded mandate. I trusted
the sickness more than I trusted my own prized inherent
difference. I trusted it more than I trusted my own voice -- my
own voice whispering through the chaos of the years as a
counterweight to this lop-sided judgment. The judgment made me
sick. My fealty to it made me sickly in my own eyes. This
unconscious decree was not mine and I could not commit to it;

neither was my individuality mine and I could not commit to
that. So I clung to this headless conformity wanting support
from it, wanting to be reconciled to it, wanting relief from it --
even though it meant conceiving of myself as a sick man; even
though it meant my sickness would be more important and
of more value than the passion for pursuing what I could be.
Can my fear of myself be so great?

THE UNKNOWN WOMAN.

Fear is the link between these gods opposed within.
Guilt and shame prepare this contest Nature preordained.
Misery decides which one eventually will win
And what is lost is suffered equally with what is gained.

THE ODDLY SHAPED MAN.

What kind of man would choose sickness as a tangible alternative
to an uncertain and unimagined future? Would choose to define
himself as sick in backward retreat from his own self-discovery?
What kind of man recoils in fear from his own values, his own
responsibilities -- his own inherent worth? A man who has
somehow become comfortable with being sick -- who has accepted
his sickness as the only final consequence of a process daring to
deviate from what was vile to him to begin with. The reason it
was vile -- the only reason -- was because it was conceived to
be universal and unequivocal; that it was in essence blindly
accepted as a truth which if unaccepted meant sickness and
deviation; deviation from a tradition demanding absolute
adherence on a specific level in a specific form. In short,
because it excluded me...

THE UNKNOWN WOMAN.

> The mystic strangers this collective god projected
> When seen subjectively can then be re-inspected.
> The first step toward a new alliance has been taken:
> His labored feeling soon with thought will be reflected;
> The slumber of its deeper image to awaken
> And cast a light upon the path the Voice directed.

THE ODDLY SHAPED MAN.

> But by logical extension who can fulfill this demand?
> Except by means of a collective illusion, the subjective nature of
> which convolutes this demand into a modified personal deviation
> on a specific level in a specific form molded to this far-flung
> general image of this inherently indescribable universal
> precept? This should be called the fiction of the ideal, the
> fiction of the universal truth. Still can I feign belief in this
> modified half-truth when I know it cannot apply to even the
> most ardent believer and supporter? The law of subjectivity
> denies its universality. The immediate experience of the individual
> makes its application impossible. This fiction is comprised of
> more unexamined aspects than my imagination can conceive. Can
> I imagine the flight of fantasies inherent in one subjective life
> experience compounded by the flight of seven billion life
> experiences compounded by the life experiences of the ancestors
> of those seven billion individuals extending back through time a
> million years and more? Could I presume to examine even a
> bare fraction of my own life experiences? Who is the deity passing
> down this unequivocal summation of humanity's life experiences?

God? Instinct? Tradition? Does living reality express itself
in the compounded subjective reactions of seven billion discrete
worlds of experience multiplied by a million years of existence
divided by Tradition over Instinct squared? Does this equal
God? Who computed this exponential equation? Who derived a
sum from this calculus containing variables not only unknown
but unknowable and even incommensurable with human
cognition? Not only unknowable and incommensurable but such by
seven billion lives times a million years and more? This is the
science of today and the "I'm sick" of tomorrow...

THE UNKNOWN WOMAN.

What a crazy welter these strange images comprise!
To thread this maze the dark opposing god is needed.
Knowledge too denies and even facts can render lies
As Nature's wisdom now from knowledge has retreated.
This power weaves its way between the foolish and the wise
And deep within this painful task is spirit seated.

THE ODDLY SHAPED MAN.

The abstraction of these ideals from the traditional course of
experience is the product of a primeval statistical equation which
science has not yet got beyond in its illusory search for wisdom -- in
its utter confusion of objective knowledge and subjective
wisdom. Normal corresponds to the degree of my submission to
this primeval ideal. This ideal is as deceptive as any
statistical picture and when suffused with personal bias --
evolves into a delusion. So it is a fact I've internalized
these certain ideas -- if indeed they were ever external at all.

It is also a fact that there were pre-existent internal ideas in me which were and are directly opposed to these also pre-existent "external" ideas. Then there should be a conflict between God, Instinct, and Tradition versus the living experience of immediate reality? Is not immediate experience the only god I can know?

THE DARK PRINCE.

It's not a flight of fancy -- it's a real opposition;
His individuality prepared its recognition.
He's stumbled on the purpose of internal tension:
To redefine and separate his thinking from the herd.
The individual is grounded in its reinvention
Of the rigid values the collective has incurred.
It's the burden of the past and the future it creates;
It puts a man at odds with what his soul relates.
Though by its own design it will ultimately lead
This man to re-evaluate the nature of his need.
But his conflict must be further etched into relief
Before he can examine it in more detail.
He must court relations with the god beneath his grief
For any chance to see the man behind the veil.

THE ODDLY SHAPED MAN.

How will I get to know you? What depth must I reach?
What fearful things will I do? What laws must I breach?
You sit in darkness hid beneath the very thought
The light of knowledge fancied it could make appear.
Indirect emotions that but half-imagined brought
Your half-imagined purposes so faintly near

Are suddenly redoubled in a flood of dark concern
For the power you've awakened through the strange veneer
Of images my thought can only half-discern.
Old unfathomed riddles lie before me still
Staring starkly at the weakness I disdain;
Mocking the illusion of my conscious will
As I yet pretend to master what I can't explain.
In fitful ways your mystery is living through me;
No wiser for it I am much less wise against it.
Are self-disdain and misery the light you've given to me
To illumine my fantasies had I but sensed it?
To cast a glow on shadow-worlds that hide your grace
From a man-child's half-perception of reality?
Who only made himself unfit for your embrace
By clinging to a make-believe morality?
All your ways frighten me I cower and evade
Yet time and again misery exceeds my fear;
And the little light in me that once a heaven made
Again must suffer its bright world to disappear.
You seemed insane though it was I who didn't understand;
I fear I'm failing still and you will lose your patience.
There seems no let in all the crazy things you've planned
To symbolize the sickness of my aberrations.
You're only guiding me I know this in my brain --
Yet what a gaping wound now bleeds within in my heart!
Though I know it's not your guidance filling me with pain
But my own desire sundering my life apart.
I can't know your purpose through the fantasies I'm seeing;
Your piercing admonitions are my only light.

If somehow I could peer inside the deep well of being
I'd surely see the marvel of my own pretentious sight.
Your monstrous grace and its privilege I must entreat
For the only useful product it creates in me;
Otherwise obscured by the harlequin of self-deceit
Ever stealing round the walls of thought's credulity.
Can I touch you in time? In mind's distant sphere?
When you tear these lovely veils of pretense from my eyes?
Will you be there? Or only darkness circumscribe my fear
And my thinking then replace you with another form of lies?
I felt you once around the corpse of my dearest friend
And somehow through my agony you gave relief;
Though just enough for me to grimly apprehend
A wondrous thing beneath my agony and grief.
I know not how these enigmatic things occur --
Your living paradox is safe from modern thought.
As stupid and unwitting as my own intentions were
I then was only following what I was taught.
I'm sorry for it now -- it was the only way I knew;
I feel its wrongness secreted within my soul.
But, for all the mystery in everything you do
I fear my misery's the only thing I know.

THE DARK PRINCE.

Through Time and effort he will soon begin to see:
What draws this image to the surface *is* his misery.
But he must step outside the circle of his Christian past
And resist his childish notions of the Devil;
For the psychic chains they represent now bind him fast

And prohibit him from searching on a deeper level.

Though he long ago pronounced such things a fairytale

They still form the basis of his valuations.

This defines the very point where intellect will fail:

The Christian myth describes emotional foundations.

THE UNKNOWN WOMAN.

Emotions come upon him from a distance so to speak;

Alien sensations in fantastic disarray.

He knows they form in the body and consciously would seek

To be rid of them for good and push them far away.

For they are most discomfiting and disconcerting;

Their unsettling appearance impedes his direction.

No more is he the subject of a mere capricious flirting

But the witless victim of their constant insurrection.

They deny his dreams of independence and control

And he must be submissive in the face of their advance.

They present a foreign threat to his imagined role

As sovereign within the realm of consciousness' expanse.

They reinforce his weaknesses and undermine his fantasies;

They confuse his picture of the world and his belief

Profoundly challenging his guarded sensibilities

From which his small defenses muster scant relief.

When he can he hides from them in cowering denial

Frantic to return to his immaculate conception;

And every intervention is a dark and painful trial

Further shaming consciousness before its self-deception.

His feigned performance suffers frequent interruption

Ever wounding him with unforeseen depressions.

A crushing misery descends with each eruption

Each time forcing consciousness to more and more concessions.

He senses it as desperation and intrusion

Unable to descry the purpose of its sorceries;

Convinced it's aberration though its regular profusion

As much describes his life as the imagined one he sees.

He can't dispense with his delusional constructions

For his projections onto culture's dark disparity:

A harsh and hostile mix of contradictory obstructions

Devised to wholly compromise a man's integrity.

His fear of these resented and disintegrative forces

Circles every act around a dark defensive element;

Ultimately measured to retard his own resources

And defend his frightened ego from his own development.

The chimera he engages in his private war

Seeks the sacrifice of fictional realities;

Fictioned tirelessly from false ideals he labored for

To escape awareness of his secret abnormalities.

These ideals are barely real enough to fix his gaze

On subjective dreams of what he thinks his life should be;

Creating his reality in convoluted ways

Yet still a fiction of his own unconscious fantasy.

This true-life fiction is the source of his confusion --

The very essence of the conflict of subjective thought:

That a man's reality is based upon illusion

And only through illusion can reality be sought.

If only one reality described the lives of men

They would still remain the beasts of Eden's paradise;

No discrimination was required of them then

The spirit weaves in opposite directions
To heal the split the conscious mind created;
And the lofty height of Intellect's projections
Must yield before these spirit-functions it evaded.

And no illusion for reality could then suffice.

But men are now the victims of a more symbolic split

Which essence is illusion and reality at once;

To discriminate between the two he must admit:

There now are *two* realities his thinking mind confronts.

If he were honest he'd embrace the Nature-given right

To contradict himself for purposes he doesn't know;

But the pattern of dishonesty yet wound around his sight

Long disabled his perception of the paradox below.

He can't discern his futile thought from any object

Or an object from a subject or the victim in between.

Such ideas are not amenable to thought and logic

For their architect lies far beyond the conscious mien.

Still the world of feeling lies behind his naked flight

From the stark antitheses of his internal state

And his imagined sovereignty must suffer every night

The unimagined offspring his imaginings create.

The Gordian knot of his unconscious compensation

Then creates a cycle of reaction and response;

And he rides this carousel in his imagination

Until he must succumb again to what this power wants.

It afflicts him for a time and he endures it as he must.

It then subsides he musters up and hopes for good it's gone;

Marvels briefly at the images reflecting his disgust --

Then at the very point he quit the ride he gets back on.

Because of his confusion he resumes the same old tread

Unobservant of the path his misery reveals.

Only stairs of starlight lit the trip through Time he led

To seek fantastic notions of his false ideals.

The glare around this path conceals the dark potential one

In the hidden universe invisible to daylight

Caught within the circle of the treadmill he must run

To keep up with the dreams his insecurities invite.

The background of his picture of the world is filled with fear:

The indirect inversion of an anxious world within.

And he is quite unable to relate to either sphere

As an unrelenting sea of feeling floods him once again.

His distorted adaptations are provisional at best;

Only further indications of an imminent descent

Through the parallel universe his miseries attest:

The unobserved and novel path of his own development...

THE DARK PRINCE.

He thinks his guilt and shame are choices he's pursuing;

As if a partial consciousness could claim its own act!

But he should know by now these darker things accruing

Seek to lead him down before a deeper world of fact.

He still views this world from consciousness' perspective:

The little part who ever thinks itself a whole.

And even though it suffers from its own objective

It still would fancy it could somehow take control;

Still would go its way as its world around it fell --

As it marveled, yet to its own fantasy would cling --

Though it lead him down before the very gates of Hell

So enticing is its fantasy to be a king...

He will see these gates of Hell and beg to be let in

When his nature deems him fit enough to see the sight.

For his misery describes his fancies from within

Just as Nature seeks to compliment each day with night.

The twinge of fear his modern consciousness conceals

At the mention of such antiquated notions

Is the means by which the ancient Deity reveals

The human history concealed in his emotions...

THE ANCIENT KING.

He feels the restless nature of the spirit-wind

Blowing where it listeth in its ancient mystery;

Whose lonely destiny and hallowed origin

Are things his earthly consciousness shall never see.

He feels as if a beast were sometime in him

More primitive than a man in Adam's day:

The great dark shadow of the star of Bethlehem --

And a modern Leviathan now in the manger lay.

He bows to lofty idols in an intimate embrace

Who for twenty centuries concealed their double-face;

And guilt and grief lay in his heart for this forbidden place

Where the spirit seeks atonement for the human race.

He yet intuits something in the stranger sense

Of a power drawing men toward their own contents:

The dark projected psychic life of unseen things –

The force beneath the waves of a man's imaginings.

This force is not the child-like god of Christian fantasy

But reaches down inside the depth of biologic man;

A place so far removed from modern vanity

It's no surprise he finds it hard to understand.

It's come pronouncing living judgment nonetheless

To try his trembling heart for Nature's dark intention;

For, the staff of misery directing his distress

Seeks to lead him to the cross of his redemption.

The wounds incurred by such enduring trials as these

Long ago compelled the ancients to the Promised Land

In tribute to a vengeful god they struggled to appease

Who yet rebuked their efforts time and time again

For the false gods and idol-worship of their former ways

Just as men are still compelled to do in modern days...

This man too proceeds toward his Promised Land;

Is likewise facing hardships with his god's demand.

This trial compels him to pursue it to the end

The vengeful side of darker gods to comprehend.

But he must sculpt the statue of traditional belief

Before he shapes the nature of his own internal grief;

And through the magic of reflection make it live again

To find the vital function it conceals within.

For this he must continue with the mythic thread

Which dark path leads into the spirits of the dead.

Historical comparisons reveal in ancient themes

The patterns of analogy in all men's dreams.

This biologic truth is what connects this man

To the living history his psyche pulses with;

And he shall be amazed when he begins to understand

How a modern mind's reflected in an ancient myth...

Part II

Coming To Terms with the Unconscious

The Inner Dialectic

The Mythic Background

The dawning awareness of the over-valuation of consciousness and the repression of the unconscious bring into question the religious/philosophical model which continues to shape even the modern scientific perspective. The unconscious seeks to move the ego aside from its assumed role of authority -- the goal of all religion -- and increase its receptivity to the demands of self-development. The intellect suffers a corresponding loss of value as the growing surge of emotional energy gains momentum. With the increasing consciousness of personal qualities in conflict with the restrictions of collective value-judgment, the deeper purposes of inner opposition begin to emerge. Symbolized in Christian imagery as the pact with the Devil, this intuitive idea takes hold as a symbol of further discrimination. The Bible states: "The Spirit bloweth where it listeth. Thou hearest the sound thereof but canst not tell whence it cometh or whither it goeth. So is every man who is born of the Spirit." The spirit in this context represents the psychic effects of evolution on the individual. Though it often creates feelings of loneliness and isolation, Erich Neumann has illustrated its greater goals to be intimately bound with those of the collective. From primitive to modern, it is the creative person who sparks cultural change. Jung wrote: Nature cares nothing for the individual yet prizes the individual above all else.

THE ODDLY SHAPED MAN.
> The process is consuming, arduous, and long
> And I fled its dark demands from the beginning.
> For, my undeveloped fantasies of right and wrong
> Only framed my conflict as another form of sinning;
> Though I was distant from the mainstream even then

And looked bewildered and confused at other men.

If they heard an inner voice I was dubious of that;

I questioned them subversively and round-about.

But their response was one-dimensional and flat

Which didn't mean they couldn't be committed and devout

But it seemed they were supported by an outer force --

Diverting both the voice's meaning and its course.

This whisper undistilled through the values of tradition

Rings very strange indeed when experienced within.

The sound of it means difference, refusal, and sedition

And the deeds that spring from it are not the deeds of most men.

I sensed it only on a superficial level --

It had forbidden echoes of a thing divine.

Somehow my heart intuited a god-like devil

Confusing even more an unsophisticated mind.

I later fought against the thought that such a thing could be

Though nonetheless was driven to its dark reality.

Certain things were not a choice as most men thought they were;

Indeed how different is seen this heady view

When mysteries and dreams and twilight things occur

In this scorching sun of consciousness the world prays to.

The inner image of my dark retreat was strange to see;

Each vision left me less enamored with the world above.

Profoundly piqued at mysteries revealed to me

I had no idea of what they were portentous of;

And they remained a banal curiosity

Until my youth was shattered by the fate of love:

Shot with a piercing dart inside a depth unknown

Leaving me exhausted, cursing, crying, and alone.

Life appeared as such a dark affliction then it seemed

If I could but endure it, it would soon relent;

Though I lacked the tools to understand the things I dreamed

Or see the secret purpose in this strange descent.

The gravity of being pressed me to my knees --

I crawled alone in filth and slime in search of clues.

But the darkness yielded not and nothing would appease

The force determining the posture I should lose.

Piece by piece my former truth was stripped and fell away

And I was naked on my knees but could not pray.

THE DARK PRINCE.

No one wills to see the netherworld this god prepared;

Even so a man must have it in his partial view.

It reflects the double-self whose nature is impaired

By what he thought he knew and knowing never knew.

He was convinced he suffered from a pathogenic brain.

He thought his healing meant the banishment of symptoms;

For to the norm the inner world will always seem insane

And doctors treat unwittingly themselves as victims.

He was ill-equipped for such a frightful revelation;

His conception of the opposites was yet too small.

His ignorance required such a dire execration

To acquaint him with a nature he could not conceive at all.

Far beyond his comprehension worked this harbinger of fate;

To his uninstructed consciousness a most unholy ghost.

All the same he sensed it in his scared and lonely state

For sickness and self-loathing had arranged to keep it close;

Unaware this anxious union would be later to create

The contact with the part of him requiring him the most.

This sick perverted part became the Deity's disguise --

The one obliterated by adult instruction:

The hallowed devil of his youth, his nature's secret prize

Brought back to life again through painful reconstruction...

He'd grown older and like all the strangers he knew then

Was too afraid to peer inside his deviation;

Cleaved to strangers' values in adapting to the world of men

To protect his thinking from his nature's own creation;

Had unwittingly observed his inherited illusion:

That its house of cards would shelter him securely in its fold;

That the wisdom of its lore would spare his dark seclusion

If he would just accept its truth and do as he was told.

He labored in the poverty of other men's desires

Until his guilt and shame exceeded his conformity.

For who could ever fathom what a deity requires

Until it brings him face to face with his deformity?

The buried dread of amputated lives unrecognized

Cast aside by conscious pride in its direction

Made dark descriptions of the future he romanticized

And strange and fearful glimpses of his self-rejection.

He saw vacant stares from soulless wraiths adrift alone

In the moral wasteland they were destined to reveal;

Where only lifeless thinking waged a battle to atone

This deep domain where birth is pain and Nature bruised his heel.

In this process thought must sacrifice its small intention;

The base of its experience is on another plane.

Its objective is to bring to trembling hearts' attention

The functions formed for Nature's purpose in a god-like brain.

These wraiths were not just victims of emotions gone astray

They were sacred vessels of a whole new point of view;

And he absorbed their functions through this natural display

Of the deaths and rebirths consciousness is subject to.

The corpses of the images consumed beneath this pall

Were changing energies in spirit's dark transitions:

Nature's means of generating life beyond the wall

Of the crippled barrenness of conscious suppositions...

He saw a stream of maiden youths in lightly flowing guise

With tender smiles and loving arms outstretched in greeting

Who as they neared grew old and gray and died before his eyes

Then down inside the underworld again receding.

He felt the cold and clutching hands emerging from his bed

Of a lifeless infant he then tried to fling away --

Horrified for his own pride to be so darkly wed

To a bride whose underside seeks only pride's decay.

This black hole of Christian soul is no-man's land indeed;

His future's vision in a single night was shattered.

The not-quite-human god of Nature spilled its seed

And idols of a thousand dreams in pieces scattered.

Men who sense it flee from it -- worship it and fear it;

Always it defies the certainty of their belief.

For those whose souls are gripped by this unconscious spirit

The sacred stone of what is known affords them no relief.

The bread from such a leaven is a hard crust to swallow

For one who ever nursed the tender teat of righteousness.

The multi-sided images are difficult to follow

For an anorexic thought brought up to worship consciousness.

He gnawed around the edges of these ceaseless interventions

Forced to taste them only by his compromised intentions.

This earthly fare will soon declare these deeper functions

Prisoned in the dark uncertainty of his presumptions.

His thought will widen out beyond his personal chagrin

To seek the burning spirit-world his nature lit within...

Behind the mundane veil of everyday obsessions

A mythic goddess weaves an age-old silhouette.

She mocks causality with shadowy impressions

Relating things he now conceives as separate.

This world is not in time with the experience

Of those for whom Reality appears with light of day.

This world prepares the future from the past's events

Through the fleeting present hiding in this interplay.

For, every riddle of the past or future shown

In the paradox of human evolution

Is in the circumstances of the present known

For the past to form the future's contribution.

New realities relentlessly becoming

Deep within the matrix of this borderline frontier

Through Nature's energy in ceaseless motion humming

Create the image of a new light to appear.

This dreaming world of symbols has intrinsic order

An undeveloped apperception cannot see.

The images emerging from this hidden quarter

In Time will demonstrate their upside-down reality.

They now produce a massive swarm of dark associations:

The chaos of creation in an undeveloped mind;

A mix of deep anxiety and sweet anticipations

As Nature seeks to implement the purpose she designed.

These new-found functions waken to a distant goal
When the I begins to look two ways at once;
And recognizes it was never in control
Of the darker vision its bright light confronts.

Which will lead him to the future he so ardently desires?

Which conspire with the changing guise of past illusions?

He was never one for faith except what honesty acquires

Which seems of little value in the face of such intrusions.

Better would he minister uncertainty and doubt;

Stop hiding from the dark unknown that fetched these riddles out

And accept his own dependence on this world of mystery --

For all his thinking made a devil of a deity!

The moral values Nature's judgment seeks to turn around

In the double-sided figures of his dreams are found.

His ears are ringing with the chorus Nietzsche spread:

"And I shall straightway turn your truth upon its head!"

Better would he search his soul and sacrifice the lad

Who inherited these images of Good and Bad;

Better yet to quit the notion he could see between the two

For Nature seeks to heal the split in this divided view.

When his single-sided conscious judgment rent these twins apart

The ego's secret fancy worked to separate his heart.

This dark nexus then became a living compensation

For unattainable ideals and their too-high temptation.

This heavenly identity is only wishful thinking --

Deep inside real demons hide in every wishful thought

Filling in the causal hole of self-indulgent seeking:

The net of chance and circumstance in which his life is caught.

This lofty system is within him whether willed or not;

It runs through each assumption like a dark motif.

It's in the veins of Western man and that's his lot

Regardless of indifference, belief, or unbelief.

Even if he claims no god his devil will remain

Deep within the symbols of this myth of self-disdain.

God's directives whisper through this shrouded mystery

And the more he flees from them the darker will they be.

His worn-out moral views are idols he projected:

The magic mirrors of his soul his thought rejected;

Caught beneath the dark unknown of conscious limitation

Holding fast the treasured past of mysteries untold

To balance out the ledger-book of god-like imitation

And cast its new reflections on these images of old...

Out of sheer necessity a devil's pact was made

For he must now supply what this man lost or squandered.

In every simple life a cosmic drama is displayed

Reflecting what the greatest minds have ever pondered.

But today there's no instruction for the blueprint of the soul;

The preachers and the scientists have failed in this respect.

No one asks or speaks of it -- no one conceives a goal

Except it imitate the herd and otherwise is suspect.

Such basic compensations would be plain to any man

Had he not slinked past the demons in his stealthy night;

Took the pains to ask his soul of his own wretched plan

For his own aloneness, hate, brutality, and spite...

A soul is useless to the herd for it's a single thing;

And when the herd pass judgment and the masses to it cling

The inner voice is silenced that a backward truth might ring

And the soul becomes a demon and the demon then a king.

THE ANCIENT KING.

Philosophy is more for those who worship what they think

Than for ones who from the goblet of uncertainty must drink.

For, many forms of thought the Western mind has stated

From the very Devil's mouth appear to be dictated.

The Christian god indeed described a heavenly sphere

Much the same as Western thought philosophized it too.

But few were driven to assess reality down here --

These weighty tasks were burdened on the Devil to do.

Such lofty schemes and dazzling dreams of empyrean height

Are peculiar to the self-inflated Western myth

Which compensates the animal and savage-like delight

Consuming everything it ever came in contact with.

This man, this thinking beast, has long the world degraded

Projecting self-rejection on the Eden God created.

Who gave this beast dominion of this earthly paradise

Only to pronounce it filthy with its own filthy vice?

The god was Western thought and its worship of itself

Who claimed this earth unfit for such a too-high beast

As would slander its own nature and anything else

Intruding on the image of this high and mighty priest.

Why else would he loathe Nature for the truth she represents

But that her acceptance was at vanity's expense?

Where are the thinkers now to plead *this* dark command

Whose demon-herd must seek it for the sake of man?

This is the legacy the Christian faith created:

That his inner nature too should be thus hated.

It shoved the Devil so far down beneath its sight

It couldn't see its own shadow for the blinding light.

Is it a wonder guilt and shame should lurk beneath the pride

Of a consciousness too unaware to look inside?

If not this compensation what describes the strange veneer

Of the two realities competing in this worldly sphere?

The beast of man's own heritage survived by Nature's hand;

It took only what its life would need for Life itself.

A man today would be aggrieved if held to that demand

For the surfeit he purloined and lavished on himself.

But his nature yet aggrieves his soul -- and this man's too --

To bargain out a consciousness from his projections.

And the Devil's grin remains within his cultured view;

Still represents atonement for these dark reflections.

For tucked away in his uncertainty and doubt

Is the unknown side of Nature's specter peering out.

The demon beast residing in this vast unknown --

The one philosophy as well is loathe to name or own --

Is the one the Western mind could never see within

And still to its dark fantasy it must pretend.

Because of this old paradox his deeds must yet confess

That God's own commandments were the Devil's nonetheless;

And still his actions suffer from the self-devoted vow

Divining sin, exalting sin, yet sin could not allow...

So this man is sore oppressed by all the things he sought

As this drama binds him faster in the myth in which he's caught.

But before the rooster crowed he denied it three times

In the dark before the rising sun of his own crimes.

But his nature soon shall manifest what he must do

For the sacrament of wine and bread is his truth too:

He shall consume his guilt before this labor's done --

A worthy sacrifice to God's neglected son.

For Peter's guilt, the prophet knew was preordained

Just as every man must own that terrible mistake.

The guilt he suffered in his night could be explained

Only through allegiance to a higher sake.

The supper he digested in those final hours

Awakened him to something greater than his grief

And he became the cornerstone of mighty powers

Spreading through the ancient world a new belief...

This man though must be content with smaller things --

It is enough if he digests his own mistake;

For the dark collective nature of this conflict springs

From an even darker god such food shall soon awake...

THE DARK PRINCE:

His soul was sold before he ever knew

Back when Adam's consciousness was just begun;

For men are ever pleased to think the things they do

Happen only when they notice they've been done.

His slavish love for the world of sense

Was only the natural consequence

Of a distant dream enforced upon his youth

Adhering more to conscious fantasy than truth.

The dream was a product of inner doubt

And the fear the Devil was seeking it out;

For indeed in his peculiar way

He breathed this myth into mortal clay.

The preachers preached and the choirs sang

To drown the dark and devilish clang

Their heathen spirits silently rang.

They hoped and prayed he was not a fact

But his silhouette peered through every act

And deeply unconscious they signed his pact.

They hurled their sins at the crucified Son

Rejoiced in the clouds for the heaven they'd won

And thought not the least of the deeds they'd done.

The fraud was worshiped and hated at once

By all who embraced such psychical stunts

As traced the confusion his mind confronts...

Where did such things originate

For a childish mind to contemplate?

Whose intuitions later grew

To question those who claimed they knew:

The God of their thought was so profound

He was not just a Dream they aspired to?

Where in the world is reality found

In this fantastic metaphysic view?

How on this *earth* is mediated

The two extremes this dream created?

How would his little world be turned about

If such ideas were ever felt to be devout?

For they spring from Nature's world of fantasy

And he has not discerned the images it paints

On the canvas of the little life he thinks is free

But yet reflects the picture of his dark restraints.

The cultural traditions he assumed were sterile

Have revealed the locus of a deeper inward search

His inner nature seeks to strip of the apparel

Of the literal translation of its symbols by the Church.

For, the notions of these values and the meaning they applaud

Are strange and antithetic to a Bible sparked ablaze

By the fearful fall into the hands of the living God

Whose fear is swallowed up by its exaggerated praise.

The convenience of such notions tends to overlook

The deeper stories illustrated in this ancient book.

The fearful thing about it he will come to understand

Is its urge for the completion of the *inner* man --

A very foreign concept to such oriented men

As were fed the partial pabulum their cultures defend;

Men who cannot tolerate a godless inclination

Yet can't accept true reverence for God's creation.

When Adam and Eve from the garden were banished

A world of objectivity completely vanished.

It still existed somewhere in the dog-eared pages

Of a heritage proclaimed by Christian sages.

Did they know better than the modern mind today?

Or were they more the victims of an ego gone astray?

THE ODDLY SHAPED MAN.

What force now begins to pull me down?

Are my own self-confessions not enough?

My mind is by an even greater tension bound

Than all my will and consciousness can yet rebuff.

I'm suddenly attacked by things I can't explain --

My sense is scattered, only images remain.

Have I dropped straightway inside my own black hole?

Is this what happens to a man who sold his soul?

The Fall into the Hands of the Living God

The devouring and disintegrating effects of the unconscious are felt as it pulls ego into the impending experience of religious drama. This natural regression is the psyche's concentration of forces as it prepares the ground for a solution to the conflicts inherent in the transformation of the conscious attitude. It is experienced as a drawing down into the depth as conscious energy is sucked into the vortex of creative unconscious activity. It is very disorienting, and as Jung remarked: if persisted in, it would result in a pathological state. It is generally interpreted by therapists today as a panic attack. This description is very accurate. It is an intense pull inward, a direct experience of unconscious demands, and it constitutes an overwhelming release of energy to the conscious mind. It is also a profound signal that these demands require further concentration and elaboration.

THE ANCIENT KING.

      When he is taken down to confront his confusion
      Through the narrow passage of the god he once created
      He free-falls through a dark world of image and illusion
      To feel the power of the God he long evaded.
      A mortal fear grips him and an overwhelming tension.
      He's trapped in this abyss, incapable of flight;
      Paralyzed by longing states in desperate suspension --
      For a time his wits are lost and he must hold on tight.
      He sees the ones he loves and who love him too
      But no kind hands reach over to assuage his fear;
      For they are apparitions, only fading from his view
      And his pleas drift into darkness for they cannot hear.

He cries in the night begging God to let him go

Imprisoned by the needful things a god can only know...

This describes the real-life world of a man's waking Dream:

The only door for thought below its otherworldly scheme.

He shall stay with it as he must for there is no release

Except he fit the images together piece by piece.

In the end this monstrous state shall dissipate his pride

And too the excess burden of the life he lives outside.

In Time his trembling mind shall thank this awful place

Releasing into consciousness the torrents of its grace.

This is how a thinking man considers how to pray;

To search for faith below the place his thought once lay.

But praying is a function in an undeveloped state --

Reflection is the conscious form his thought must liberate.

And faith is not yet quite enough to reach the Promised Land;

He must now reflect on what created this demand.

He then may realize: the things for which he pleaded

Are not identical with what his nature needed.

From it springs the fearful things of which the Bible spoke:

The living spirit scatters madness at a single stroke.

This is why men's reason fails before an all-good God

And must defend ferociously its heavenly facade.

They pander superstition and the worst inanity

That Christ should bear the burdens of the crosses meant for men.

Who in madness ever pondered his own sanity

Any more than ancient rabbis questioned themselves then?

Whose crucifixion shall the Second Coming come to see

But the trembling heart whose inner man is struggling to be?

Archetypal Roman soldiers walk the earth today

Though their crucifixions have been secreted away;

Nailed upon their phobias, compulsions, and depressions –

Like this man -- upon the cross of consciousness' obsessions.

THE UNKNOWN WOMAN.

When his nature freed him from this intimate domain

He'd been deluged with a flood of feeling through his brain.

The wraiths of his loved ones in this fathomless abyss

Were the idols of his fealty to his own consciousness.

These images intruded their creative state

To draw attention to the needs they compensate:

He'd flown to the stars and back on his philosophic notions

And in falling he hit hard on the ground of his emotions.

He could not escape it, there was nothing he could do --

The fear and panic of a primitive was all he knew.

It was the naked energy of his unconscious task

Flooding him with future forms his thinking couldn't grasp.

He can't conceive them yet, his eyes are still half-closed

Though when he wakes, a stranger world will slowly be exposed:

A world of greater magnitude than daylight's little glow;

Far beyond the boundaries an intellect can know.

Even in his drowsy state with gratitude he seeks

The searing pain of undesired tears upon his cheeks.

This pain of achievement in a struggle long endured

Is the gift of recognizing he could still be cured

Of the modern-day affliction of a partial dream

Which conceives its own reality to be supreme...

The real test, however, has yet to be faced:

When dead things are buried they must be replaced.

The struggle must continue on a higher plane --

And a man must resurrect a god when it is slain.

THE ODDLY SHAPED MAN.

Only something quite remarkable could cause all this!

How could I have ever guessed the spirit worked this way?

I saw many pictures in my dreams of the abyss

But never outright in the open light of day.

Why me? is a question I have come to live with;

It seems I had a devil in me from the start.

I just never noted he was only half the myth

Or a double-god might show its presence in my heart.

Only yet a peek before it slipped away again

To change its shape as soon as I had seen the sight.

Just when I had peered inside a hidden spirit-land

It drew the inner veil and took away the light...

Is it really so the secret pact I signed

Many years ago when I was but a youth?

Or is it just the crazy notion in my mind

That even gods and devils might be only half the truth?

THE ANCIENT KING.

So Time has degraded the gods he once knew

And created consciousness for something new.

He can't know what it is: it doesn't work like that.

If the mighty thrones on which the old gods sat

Were as perishable as human thought

Then who would bear the burdens the Bible taught?

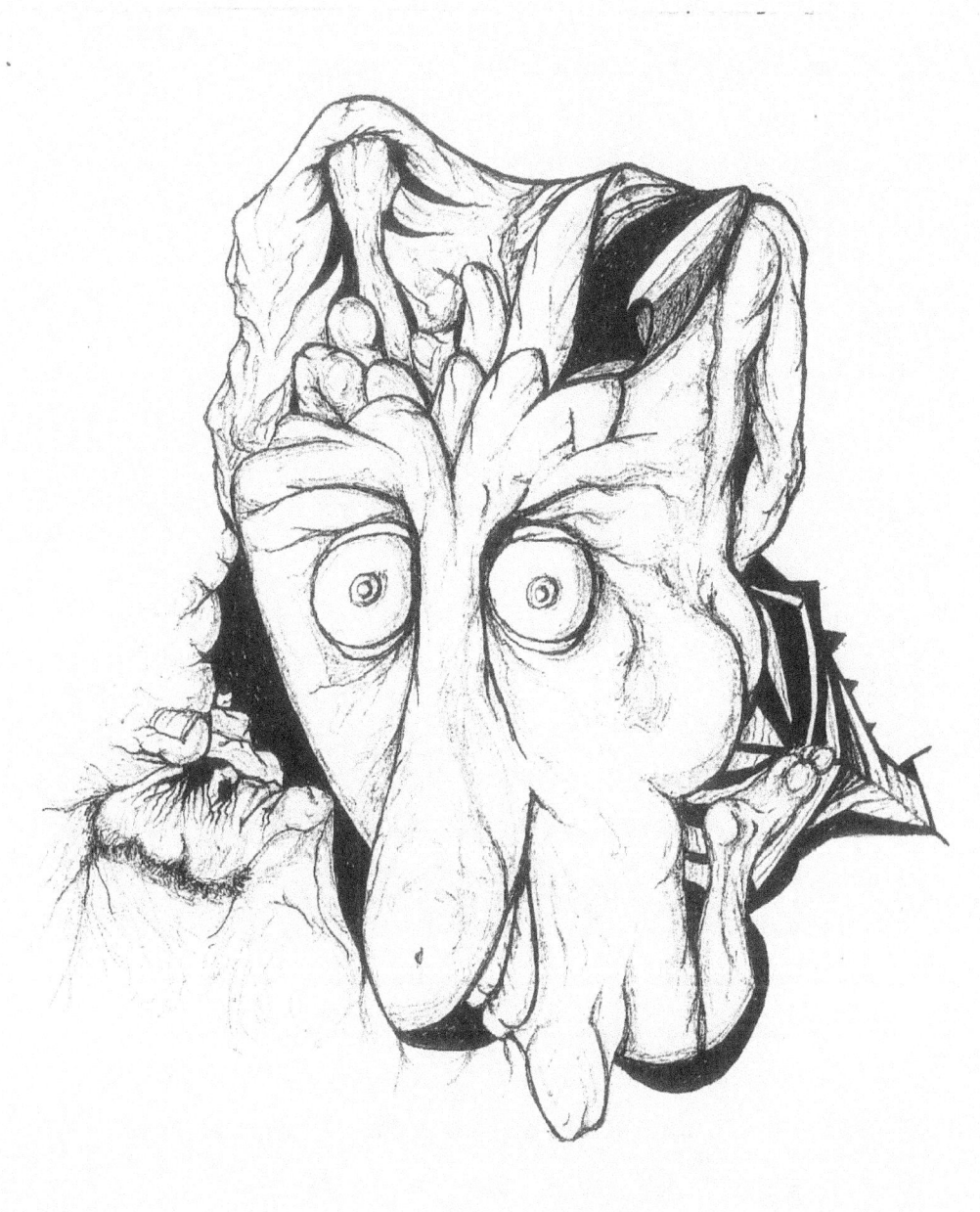

The spirit's wound will slowly come to surface
And beneath its urges, stranger forms appear
As the inner man concealed in the abyss
Births himself through conflicts represented here.

For a man's thought shifts from hour to hour
Directed by forces beyond his power.
Would he will the growth of his own tissue
After solemnly thinking on the issue?
Would the evolution of life ensue
Only when a man had thought things through?
This divine force whatever he thinks it is
Lives its own dark life far apart from his.
If he's determined to bring it nearer
He must gaze in a deeper mirror:
Not the one revealing his small face
But the one reflecting the human race;
For he is what he is and shall always be
An Image in the mirror of this Deity...
Through such limitations each modern man gives in
To the upside-down values of the world he lives in.
They describe a thinking mind whose truth is in retreat
From the dictates of a force below it so discreet
It can't be seen but through the symbols it expresses --
In a consciousness whose images its thought represses.
So he needs acceptance from the only world he knows
To spare him from the lonely wind the ancient spirit blows.
These values are the safest certainty he's ever known
And only a confused uncertain head could drive him on.
He never chose these things nor shall he heal the open wound
Inflicted by this strange uncertain world his soul attuned.
Beneath the twisted edict of the outer contradiction
Lives this deeper universe demanding his conviction.

Thus between the stranded strait of known and unknown

This man must navigate the double-world in which he's thrown.

One might as well question how life was created

As to ask such a man how his heart had been invaded.

These things just happen to a man and he obeys them;

Only his own soul shall name the price he pays them.

Nature has ordained it though he knows or not

And if she wills he shall be dead upon the spot.

But only if his attitude opposes her decrees

For men are subject to her in mysterious degrees.

If his fate determines he shall seek another course

And allows him to escape an early death

He must yield his heart to this objective force

Just as he depends upon his own breath.

THE DARK PRINCE.

It's a painful task to leave such things behind

As built the hallowed halls of the collective mind.

When a man is forced to seek a dark unknown

He labors in his difficulties all alone.

This drives him ever further into isolation

From the friendly comforts culture once projected

Coercing him to seek a new relation

With the *real* disease with which he is infected.

The process is perceived in this peculiar way

Because he can't conceive the inner man straightway.

A consciousness is built upon in stages:

Just as men have been compelled throughout the ages

To step-by-step concede a world of fantasy

His torpid thought but slowly disengages

From a consciousness that turns around reality.

THE UNKNOWN WOMAN.

A man's philosophy is crafted through emotion

The base of which is laid by his peculiar fate;

And through the shadow-side of personal devotion

Describes in images the feelings they create.

His thought has less to do with conscious reasoning

Than his philosophy admits however chaste.

For every recipe is sprinkled with the seasoning

Each dish requires to appeal to his own taste.

What philosopher can think outside his hallowed head

To acknowledge something he cannot believe?

And ordain for men his own unleavened bread

Except he judge what his own thought could not conceive?

Saul saw in Christians what his own mind projected:

The secret nature of his soul his thinking had repressed;

Until his fate prescribed for him what he rejected

And Paul was turned around by what his soul expressed.

Such examples of conversion serve to illustrate

The image all men's feelings seek to compensate:

Such preconceived philosophies as must believe

In only what their partial thinking can achieve...

Can he not see his misery as his projected fate

Soaring into distant realms his soul to compensate?

Is it not the same collective Christian clothing

Of the Sunday suit and tie of his self-loathing?

Is it not the hubris of his philosophic thought

Exposing the Leviathan the scriptures taught?

Like Job's dialectic with God's hidden might

It is an honest man's search for his own inner light.

Job couldn't draw Leviathan out as with an hook

For his own dark reliance on the rules in the book.

It then became the need for God to take him down

To manifest the beast his culture tried to drown;

And its truth too was God and when he turned around

Was humbled by the spiritual conflict he found.

THE DARK PRINCE.

It was Satan who moved the Lord to test Job's heart;

And Jehovah struck a deal with the Devil too.

Even gods are turned around by Lucifer's art

For the sake of the light men thought they knew...

This turn-around though is not the surface task it seems;

Its implications lead to more than he detects.

Already he's discovered in the nature of his dreams

A picture far beyond what consciousness suspects;

Indeed had summed his life up in a single scene

If his partial thought could comprehend its symbols.

But the dressed-up mystery behind the subtle screen

Of the darker images his inner world resembles

Only yields the deeper pictures of its hidden past

In the blackest shadows of the modern light they cast.

"Ask and ye shall be given" -- "Seek and ye shall find" --

Simple words enough if one is biblically inclined;

Though such notions bear the heavy weight of centuries --

Many men have died for simple phrases such as these.

So too a man's own dreams are burdened with this weight;

Each image dreamt must far exceed what words relate.

This unassuming concept of turning around

Only through emotional experience is found.

THE ANCIENT KING.

His fancied thought betrays this born-again trend

Forever in danger of losing the thread.

Such a man shall go down again and again

To compensate the image that inflates his head.

Such ideas are not reflective of the little men they seize --

The pipers he must pay to know them are legion indeed.

Their dark collective nature seeks false gods to please

Whose masks are dedicate only to collective need.

They wander mapless in a strange and foreign land;

Ever so seductively they lead a man astray.

He may think he strolls with God in Eden hand in hand

But when he looks more closely only devils slip away.

They convince him he sits perched atop a lofty throne --

That upon his little head a golden crown adorns;

Only then to cast him down before a dark unknown

And spin his haloed fantasy around a crown with horns.

Their human need is only surfacely apparent --

A beastly aspect overshadows their ideals;

And the brutish tendencies remain inherent

In the undeveloped soul this ape conceals.

Yet these legion pipers in this strange and foreign land

Hide in turn the nature of an even stranger man

Who fought for eons to evolve the modern shape

Of the older beast within this lofty thinking ape.

Inside a century these thinking apes would slap your face

At such ideas of heritage from a primitive race;

Though now they've half accepted it they still can't comprehend

The reasons why the human animal shall yet descend...

But a man's descent is combined with his ascension

To reconcile the double-world behind the Devil's cloak.

It gives the depth he needs for consciousness' extension:

His only chance to grasp the hook of which Jehovah spoke.

But grievous conflicts ever mark the path of this descent;

For a man cannot be sure which truth to recognize

When a mythic beast informs him of his discontent

And lofty images have since turned into lies.

This hook delves far below his scientific thought

To a *human* depth in which this animal is caught.

The paradox his modern hope is wedged between

Is the one beyond the microscope: the spirit gene.

THE ODDLY SHAPED MAN.

What are these murky shadows I now see

Peering through the curtain I once thought was me?

I surely rent these garments long ago --

They were the reasons I once sold my soul.

How is it they so stubborn have returned

In the modern-day disguise of what I've learned?

THE DARK PRINCE.

Divided thinking leads at last to conflicting goals:

To the two-way mirrors in the depth of all men's souls;

Reflecting dual minds in which the opposites prevail
Yet only one can be observed through the conscious veil.
Even in the lofty labs of science this exists
Its subjective basis proven by the physicists:
The uncertain observations Heisenberg asserted
Were the limitations of their minds their thought perverted;
Though even these do not reflect the dark uncertain forms
Imposed by thought's restriction to objective norms.
The conditions of the soul determine what men seek
The probable statistics are a modern double-speak.
What natural reality makes any sense at all
Without a concept of the purposes inherent in it?
Life would never have arisen on this earthly ball
Without the spirit everywhere apparent in it.
The faithful picture of the world such concepts have defined
Still are psychic products with conditions of their own;
And symbols weave their purpose through the conscious mind
In the secret depth to which itself remains unknown.
The uncertain relativity of modern science --
The deepest of realities the mind has yet discerned --
From the smallest particle to planetary giants
Reflects as well its two-way mirror when the glass is turned.
Such ideas are not conceived as psychic intuition
Though perceived to be the ground reality requires.
Even physics can't escape the basis of cognition
Revealing inner aspects of the knowledge it acquires.
Through these secrets half-described in man's imagination
Spirit, too, participates in matter's dark foundation.
Nature's secrets are elusive as her properties require --

Most of all within the matter of the soul's desire.

The truths in her images the scientists have won

Lead below the world of things inside a deeper one.

Faust said long ago, "Two souls are dwelling in my breast" --

Now a proven fact the oldest atom will attest.

At the same time as Einstein a Swiss psychologist

Informed objective science of the very thing it missed:

The subjective factor – provable empirically --

Was a psychic analogue for space-time relativity.

This factor hides a deeper law than instruments reveal

For the law of man's being is a factor he must feel...

Alas two psychic truths are dwelling in his head

Based on opposition like the physicists said.

"Each is feign to leave its brother," just as Faust opined;

And one denied the other for the concepts it divined.

The older one -- the matrix men's awareness can't concede --

Is the very god-likeness their consciousness decreed

As an image of themselves and the wonders they begat

Perverting their own reason as a price for that.

A deeper opposition yet resides within

The partial values in the minds of thinking men:

Like salesmen they construct a future shopping mall

At the same time hoarding weapons to destroy it all...

Men are only objects in these dark imaginings;

Themselves reduced to ciphers in a world of Things.

What man if he had ever drunk from spirit's well

Could quench his thirst with the technologic brew they sell?

Are the scientific prophets merely profiteers?

What human soul has been enhanced by their inventions?

Strange desires cloud the lens through which this science peers:

The *subject* of the object now confuses its intentions;

Though men are left to struggle with the same old human fears

As once claimed Eve's and Adam's and the snake's attentions.

No problem is beyond this objective human quest

Except the small subjective one in a man's own breast;

Yet still all forms of superstition will suffice

To convince him of his distance from his own inner vice.

This same collective border Christianity constructed

Repels a man from seeking what his nature has to say.

Though now it's on the other side of heaven life's conducted

It has still the same objective to explain the world away

And only understand enough to serve the greed created

By the hallowed histories of pious people long since gone;

Driven still by inner forces Nature arbitrated

That science and religion both have turned their backs upon...

For this man to free his mind he must consider things

Quite the opposite the paradigm instilled in him;

For the intellect inflames a man with waxen wings

Soaring far beyond the nature being willed in him.

This will is not his own and not obsessed with other men

But strives below the known to seek a world within;

For the re-creation of an older mystery

And he is only driven there by hard necessity.

He views his thinking through the glass of self-importance;

The wonders he beholds are mystical possessions.

They bewitch and stupefy in mythical accordance

With the ancient laws established by a man's obsessions.

A man must have a counterweight to these Platonic spheres

Like giant shadows crouched behind his small and modest fears.

He loves these fears too in his own clandestine way:

Such is the bargain struck by men who cannot pray.

He barters spirit-life for dark and fleeting pleasures

To flatter only Image's obsessive measures.

But a man who cannot pray must worship nonetheless

The gods of his disorders whom his fantasies confess.

Such are the idols of a space-age mythology

Until recently the ones the heavens once concealed;

Now the orphans of a modern-day psychology

Yet not much less divine and not much more revealed.

For gods have ever issued from this psychic netherland

In any form interpreted to make men understand

That a greater spirit hides within the human mind

Than by science or the intellect will ever be defined.

But the prophets of today are focused on the brain

Able only to connect with what they touch and see.

No man yet has seen a god in the physical domain

Except the demons lurking in the body's chemistry.

The gods are demons now to this enlightened man

Whose only world consists of what his thought can understand.

The psychic history on which his life is based

By the shining light of Consciousness is now erased.

What was once a sacred sphere by which this man was graced

Has been reduced to symptoms and by chemicals replaced.

What once were ancient deities have now become disease --

Their double-nature no objective science can appease.

How could such a troubled culture now have come about

But that its egotism turned its thinking inside-out?

Denied the things its own spirit thundered long ago
For self-deceptive mysteries its science couldn't know.
A bi-polar syndrome underlies the Western mind
For these neglected opposites are moving to the fore;
Just as they comprise the nature science has defined
So also do they form the nature scientists ignore.
They force a man inside himself though willed or not;
They urge him to consider things his modern mind forgot.
They sometimes even make him pray though on a thinking level
Not the least discernible from praying to the Devil.
He's the hidden opposite of the rational mind
Tucked behind the Christian image thinking men defined.
His emotionality provokes instinctive fear
Of the symptomatic function grinning through his ancient leer...
Every man's affliction is exposed in special form
That his thought's addiction might discover Nature's needs:
There is a part of him indeed which seeks beyond the norm
To lead him to an inner truth the outer one impedes.

THE UNKNOWN WOMAN.

Emotions long opposed him as they do with thinking men
And they still comprise the darkness he must struggle in;
Though his male-centered viewpoint once stuck to the norm
Now attacks his consciousness in more symbolic form.
Feeling is a vital function he no more disputes;
No longer can he see it as the weak display
Embodied by an angry world of frightened brutes
Who early sent his life so terribly astray.
The smaller issues in that world he struggled with

Have now descended deep inside a world of myth.

This antithesis imposes less apparent fears

Than the worldly compensations of his younger years.

His fear is not of weakness in the face of men

But the shadow-force behind their caricatures;

And the feelings emanating from this world within

Send him fleeing ever back to Thought's seductive lures:

Where man-made idols seek their sacred right as kings

To wish away the misery he still endures;

For he's not discovered yet: his lonely sufferings

Are compelled by what this image still obscures.

It demands he search these shadow-gods in novel ways --

A deeper recognition of the world beyond his thought;

Acceptance of the antinomies consciousness betrays

To relieve him of the ancient myths his fathers taught:

Such are men in whose images the gods were made

And in desperation from the other side they hide.

They set no limitations in their grand charade

To cover the inferiority they feel inside.

Many men labor with such disconnected notions

And their preconditions are the stunting of emotions.

In his primer to the study of such psychic laws

He still gropes in darkness for a personal cause;

Unwitting that the paradox of self-disdain

Now stares back at him from a religious plane...

The gods and goddesses demanding his attention

Are the male and female wraiths of thought and feeling;

Another step toward the task of reinvention

Of the stranger world these symbols are revealing.

The great wide sphere of confrontation in his youth

Reveals inside as well a dark collective truth.

It unveils an opposition to his thought's facade

Feeling can interpret only as the will of God.

Far beyond the lonely pleas exhibited before

This god requires real work to pierce its mythic lore.

His prayers will not relieve him of his self-rejection

Anymore than faith can substitute reflection.

Through this sphinx's riddle he may yet become a king

Though not the sort his lofty thinking once constructed.

Such royalty is found in the depth of his being

And it is there where consciousness will be instructed.

The problems in these depths are fraught with superstition

For those compelled by their seductive introversion

To weave some sort of sense around their split condition

And find an answer to this hallowed self-aversion...

THE DARK PRINCE.

His split condition slumbers in his lordly attitude:

The one his inner nature seeks to turn around.

For this he will be re-acquainted with the ancient feud

Once prophesying Lucifer to be cast down.

At that time the Shining One still had a human face

Though through the centuries his nature has regressed;

Now too dark and far away for the embrace

Of a consciousness with artificial things obsessed.

Yet his deeper function no man may erase

But only turn around the opposites expressed

When human value judgment sacrificed the grace

Of the living world of Nature then repressed.

Whose partial thought created what he feels today?

Whose lofty god once heralded salvation?

The one whose inner darkness stole the light away?

The same one now who forms the Spirit of Negation?

THE ANCIENT KING.

He feels lost now and utterly forsaken;

His little faith and all his knowledge deeply shaken.

He feels the beastly side of Nature's inner man:

The animal imprisoned by the Christian god's command;

Himself risen to dispute Christ's resurrection

And breathe inside the myth a powerful correction.

One he neither wills nor is prepared to understand --

His buried soul now fallen down inside a pagan hand.

It's the left hand of God made evil by repression;

Feared, debased, and left to form a dark obsession.

The ape of God is born again within his soul

To redeem its own nature from the Christian horde;

To implement the process of becoming whole

And compensate the inner man theology ignored.

This godly ape has lain in chains for too long now.

His resurrection is an answer to the Christian vow:

It parted man's internal world like Moses split the sea

Fashioning the age-old wall of Christianity.

It's Nature's response to kingdoms not of this world:

The inner image of the one men seized dominion of

As strange and fertile spirits through the deepest reaches swirled

With the teeming doubts beneath the Christian mask of love.

The hidden doubts concealed in this forbidden space
Are natural components humankind cannot replace;
But only sacrifice the misery sublime
First interpreting the act of Eden's crime:
When the snake forced men from their paradisal place
They substituted Nature with their own rejected face.
This lofty usurpation left them all alone
With a world of animals they struggled to replace;
To consider how a conscious nature could atone
The strange development effecting this disgrace...
The double-face of these old images of guilt and sin
Comprises still the tension of the opposites within
The very beast whom Nature sought through such duress
To become the living vessel of her own consciousness.
Thus at once he was afflicted with disgrace and pride
As a symbol of the conflict Nature birthed inside.
He was never capable to see this on his own
Anymore than any beast who faced the dark unknown;
And Nature undertook her timely task again
To resurrect more symbols for the beast to understand.
But they only served to make him fall in love the more
With an even more self-flattered image than the one before...

The Hidden Passion of a Lost Anxiety

The religious drama begins to unfold on a subjective level through the symbol of Christ's crucifixion and its relation to modern consciousness. As a psychic analogy, it represents the emotional tension of functions intended to create individual solutions to developmental conflicts in the collective unconscious. Christ represented a deep mythic response to the primitive spiritual conditions in antiquity. Today, our changing natures are reflected in division, diversion, disorientation, suggestibility, a longing to adhere to a cause or "ism" or to be contained within the security of a social, political, or religious system which no longer serves the aims of psychic development. Traditional symbols and their interpretations are quickly losing relevance, and the older orientation becomes increasingly ineffective as a check against our animal natures. The "beast within" must be re-interpreted to stimulate a new image which would more adequately express the changing relations with the unconscious. Without its symbols to attract consciousness to goals beyond its own desires, the deeper designs of instinct are projected onto external circumstances and often lead to the violent acting out of what is ultimately a psychological/spiritual conflict.

why hast thou forsaken me? he screamed from the cross of
his physical suffering;
as the life in his body was painfully stripped away.
as the legions of onlookers gaped at the frightening sight
many cheered, lauding the grisly scene.
yet all were afflicted -- even the oddly shaped man in his
chair smoking his cigarette.
what a shame he thought as the smoke circled about his
head: that there should be such suffering in that world.
he crossed his legs and stared pensively at the austere furnishings.

the shouts of the multitude drifted away with the smoke

he had just exhaled.

he considered in silence the earthly vision and felt empty.

most of the ghostly onlookers trailed away in the foggy aftermath.

the cross stood bare then -- a monument weighing heavily on the

lives of the few who remained;

those spectators of history who would re-enact the spectacle

in their own souls for generations to come;

would feed on the image ravenous in their hearts for a piece of it.

later – the well-meaning multitude would define it inwardly as a new

form of greed.

they would bear the icon proudly as an unconscious symbol

of their own inner violence.

eventually the symbol tightened about their necks choking back

the fear coursing through their trembling bodies.

they were yet mindful of the divine catastrophe even as their

heads gradually lifted from their shoulders --

muted ears grown into wings large and flapping as their

trembling bodies twitched and withered and attenuated.

the large wings flapped the head away into thin air and it

became smaller and smaller as it floated into the stratosphere.

the empty eden thus returned to its innocence and new lives were

begun anent its sufferings.

the multitude of disembodied heads cast an occasional glance at the

empty eden that was once a living reminder –

but it registered only as faded pages in an antique book.

they lamented their anorexic bodies at times but the thrill of flying

exceeded the remote memories of that toilsome earth-bound world.

for the withered bodies had done shameful things -- on their own;

had so disgusted their vanities that the winged heads deigned not
to descend from their cyber-spheres;
and their dissociated machinations swirled them steadily
to new spiritual heights.
the oddly shaped man in his chair sat silently still, listening
to these new spiritual heights clatter noisily in the street
outside his window.
the rays of light illumined the cloudy formations in sharply
defined borders piercing into his twilit room.
he thought how lonely he was as he squatted beneath this loving
god who had sacrificed his children's bodies that they might
revel so convinced in the blessings of his lofty world.
he could scarce contain the guilt and shame he felt for those
spiritual gifts as the smoke haloed round his head.

THE UNKNOWN WOMAN.

His slowly turning thought is more confused than ever
The path becoming less familiar now with every turn;
For the empty Eden has revealed the dark endeavor
Of the ever-changing symbols he must now discern.
They'll soon replace a dogma with the needs of the abyss
Whose looming nature grows more threatening with each attempt
To pierce the foggy images his mind cannot dismiss
And open up the riddle of his grief and self-contempt.
They are being animated now to fill the space
Of the fear excited by his criminal regard
For the greater mystery in this forbidden place
Which seeks the frightened little man he must discard.
The fear inherent in this process is the child

Of the fantasies his culture once conceived:
Where every man becomes the god his ego styled
And in its realm no other idol is believed...
This man understands: a rival has possessed him
Who seeks to take away the crown of his belief.
He knows this rival has degraded and depressed him;
Found his once-grand life to be deflated by its grief.
For when this process seized him he was forced to answer it
Its relentless mystery no longer could allay.
But fight it as he might, within his heart he must admit:
The fantasies of ego-gods just will not go away.
But such a process isn't bound by thought's direction;
It portends what it will do according to its need.
This can only be determined by intense inspection
Of contradicting images his thought must learn to read.
They will surface slowly as his gods are broken down --
Just as they advanced from their inglorious beginning --
When he reflects upon the simple grains of truth he found
In the older forms of his own nakedness and sinning.
On a higher level still they soon will be repeated
As they transform before a new experience --
And each succeeding fantasy is superseded
By the rival seeking meaning in his deviance...

THE ODDLY SHAPED MAN.

Suddenly I'm taken back to long ago:
To the marble statues of my lost and lonely lust;
Yet straining now to see through time's elusive flow
Even those old pillars only half-way turned to dust.

I gave up for them one god upon another
To search for something hidden in my desperation;
Only in my dark confusion to discover
I seem no closer to my longed-for destination.
Their form has changed, it's true -- half-ethereal in shape;
But that's a problem too, for bodies I still see
Swirling round me in the images I gape
Fighting still with ancient spirits to be free.
If bodies to the spirit are so indisposed
Why are spirit's dreams revolving round them so?
How do they cling fast when they are so opposed --
Who pronounced them enemies so long ago?
What dark and unseen form lies in between the two
Binding them despite their mutual disgusts?
What kind of crazy god is this I'm fettered to
Who at once two contradicting worlds upon me thrusts?
The things I long denied between my irreligious youth
And the later things implied by my compulsive deeds
Somehow work to fashion a cohesive truth
From what the spirit seeks and what the body needs.
Surely the desires of the two must somewhere meet
And I search now the storied past of where they would
In the only source of history where men entreat
A God they later claimed to represent the Good --
But once around his throne the Evil One did seat.
The latter must analogize my golden calf:
The older one who deems my soul still incomplete
For the Christian god who split my world in half
And left me pleading now at his uneven feet.

Swirling images of bodies from the deep
Reflect the heritage a man is burdened with.
Through every individual these shadows creep
Behind the ancient background of its myth.

I try with all my might to put the pieces back

In a form acceptable to both for what they lack.

But the more I try the more I'm torn apart

By these two opposing forces in my heart.

If the spirit once was hidden in the body's urge

Must not the body and the spirit somewhere merge?

Yet in a form the ancient scripture, too, divided

From a single image once by Nature guided?

Whose opposed powers only later duplicated

The split reflections in the beast she then created?

THE DARK PRINCE.

At last he's driven to religious inquiries

For these ideas exert a powerful attraction.

Despite the drama of his past soliloquies --

Where to the intellect they represent distraction --

Deep within this force is found the source of his disease

Which forms the hidden counter-pole to thought's reaction.

But he had joined league with Mephisto in his youth

Never then suspecting lies could somehow form the truth;

For he possessed a blinding urge to criticize

Too concrete to find the truth between the lies.

Though inspired by the urge for truth he labored on

In a world of fact entwined with superstition;

Yet unable to interpret the unknown

That lay beneath the values of tradition.

And in his zeal and ignorance he swept away

All the subtleties both truth and lies betray.

His truth will be difficult to find no doubt;

He was never chosen for the faith of the devout.

He could always see beneath the mask of others' lies;

Could lord the misconceptions of the uncouth.

All these things he trained himself to recognize --

But can he see the contradictions in his own truth?

This truth issues from the same objective source

Where Nature's dreams seek answers for the darkest need

As they thread connections through the winding course

Of the serpentine direction on the path they lead.

They form the old caduceus of the inner way

From images of Instinct's perilous travails.

As in ancient men they worked they work today

To forge realities from their subjective tales...

Such ideas of bodies, creatures, devils, and beasts

Are aspects of an image he can't quite conceive;

Yet whose contrast to the holy ghosts of godly priests

Darkly illustrates the strange relationships they weave.

These are not apparent to a mind who must personify

The energies inherent in the seeds of Nature's growth;

So the thinking part in its attempts to quantify

Must learn to factor in the energies of both:

The earthly aspects are religious compensations

For the dwelling place of deities without a ground;

And this man's feet can no more tread on speculations

In the sphere of thought he once deemed so profound.

His nature now requires him to reappraise

The high-flown knowledge of the attitude he prizes;

As he is swept by Nature's solitary gaze

Through a world of fact his thought but barely recognizes...

No creature yet has walked the earth with wings upon its feet

Nor one that flew, from earth's reality has been released.

Not a thing that slithers, runs, or flies however fleet

Yet escaped the living nature of a worldly beast.

Until he finds the strength to face *that* force inside

The compensations for his little god remain.

His contest with the ancient beast must now decide

How far his healing will incorporate his pain.

His own caduceus verifies this crazy course

Weaving still between the spirit's double-speak --

For him to be acquainted with the shadow-force

Which will mediate the healing he must seek.

THE ANCIENT KING.

In his twisted thinking he must come to understand:

The values of the Church have slain the soul of Western man.

The soul's flicker is extinguished in the social urge --

The rejected sense of self becomes collective scourge --

And the secret sorcery of evolution's thrust

Becomes a magic only individuals can trust.

The rest are left to plead to a distant psychic force

Which scatters broken lives like cosmic debris;

Yet always gravitates around the hidden source

Of the individual's inherent mystery.

The churchly sense of power and divine law

Genuflected only to its own self-awe

And hid beneath the Church's mighty sway

The subtle course of the soul's inner way.

It brutalized and conquered whole foreign lands

For the savage doubts that trembled in its childish heart;
And men's appeals to God were only the demands
Of the insecurities which ripped a world apart;
Their greed a hollow testament to what they'd always been
Despite the loving Jesus they concocted in their minds;
Whom their egos half-created to relieve them of their sin
Yet only found them mired deeper in their own designs...
The Romans never changed with Christianity
Nor did the German hordes nor anybody else
Who sacrificed the Nature of their own humanity:
A dark unconscious picture of their god's internal stealth.
The ancient beast the Christian world assumed it left behind
Lives in the collective values of the modern mind.
The echoes of this banished beast still sore oppress
The soul of each small man in his unconsciousness.
Such collective values long have rendered upside-down
The symbols of the inner man for his attention;
And the consequence of his neglect is so profound
He turns into its opposite the holiest intention...

A Late Night Commercial Message

The urge to wholeness increases the pressure to reconcile the intellect with its collective emotional foundations by moving the two into ever closer proximity. Spontaneous fantasies inform consciousness with hints of their symbolic intent through the broader analogies of science and religion. The historical psyche expresses itself through its collective nature to provoke individual responses to social conditions. With focus and devotion, this process has the paradoxical effect of contracting and expanding consciousness at the same

time. It draws conscious energy inward through the fascination of its images,
deepening the exchange with the unconscious, as it also lays the groundwork
for the emotional and spiritual connections which would bind the individual to
the greater needs of humanity.

The discreet council of forgotten gods wept silently
Grieving for the false atonements they'd disseminated.
Fantastic notions in their children circled violently
Around the prototypes the gods themselves created.
The old paradox of scripture threatened universal flood --
Waters stirred by ancient tomes the neophytes translated.
Science studied excrement and preachers pondered blood
As they cracked the core of images the gods re-stated.
Bred consumers gazed at the dream but soon became bored
As the soft glow of their diversions lit the tranquil night;
Though jesters praised the neon signs interpreting the Lord
And youngsters gathered at their feet to celebrate the sight.
Few bothered with the spectacle and even fewer guessed
That a brand new vision of the Trinity had risen
From the unaccounted dogma beggars laid to rest
Which centuries before had formed the spirit's prison.

THE DARK PRINCE.

Hid behind this neon sign is advertised the quest
Of holding thought accountable to Nature's standard.
Though new ideas of God will shortly be undressed
Just how they fit with older ones has not been answered...
Such obscure messages and their confusing dread
Contain analogies his cloudy thought can scarcely know

Until a clearer image can ascend within his head

To inform him of the process working down below.

But for now the process reckons from the other end

To defecate the psychic toxins he ingested;

To relieve him of the fantasies of other men

Along with all the strange emotions they arrested.

It's an ancient concept hidden deep within his bowels:

The paradox of opposites in natural creation.

It hides the earthly treasure his collective thought befouls

In the deeper realm of spirit's operation.

It's the little dung-hill modern men despise;

It yields the gold his thinking has rejected.

Though far a man may search it always lies

Concealed within the image he projected.

While all unconscious contents seek the light

Only Nature will decide where they appear;

And she cares nothing whether men approve the site

For she functions through the body and her truths lie here...

A Modern Creation Myth

The undifferentiated psyche often analogizes mental events through the body's functions, just as primitive rites and rituals symbolized instinctual functions which later emerged as psychological ideas. My five year-old niece once pulled me excitedly into the bathroom after her bowel movement, "Look what I did!" she proudly exclaimed. This is a primitive analogy of having produced or given birth to a new psychic product. It also contains the opposite idea: the letting go of "waste" or that which has become a hindrance to the development of the new attitude toward which the unconscious is aiming.

He was so covered with shit he scarce could draw a breath.

It was meant to protect him -- this shit-covered mask.

Instead it has restricted and confined him to the depth

Where beneath its dung-heap lies the object of his task.

It was meant to guide him smoothly through the streaming flow

Of all the shit-faced strangers who had perished long ago;

Who themselves were buried by the silent steaming turds

Their bodies heaved for centuries beneath their Christian words.

They defecated secretly their Eden's innocence

On the twisted faces of their children for the truths they swore;

Diversions for their lonely lives in ways he couldn't sense

Until the god of Nature spilled the burden they both bore.

His face and hands were smothered with the sewage it expelled.

His feet were soiled in a noxious cloud of burnt desires;

Stifling and pungent through the stinking smoke they smelled

His shit-stained mouth pretending smiles behind the fires.

Drunken from the soured wine that puked the love they held --

Frightened by the smoke arising from their covenants --

He was frightened more by what those ancient deeds compelled

In this god of Nature's unrevealed requirements.

THE DARK PRINCE.

This cloud veils the image of the treasure it possesses;

The unimagined one his thinking still represses:

The process he could not conceive and feared with half his heart

But one whose other half was pressed upon him from the start.

The former deity his nakedness had once concealed

Before his youth was shattered by his lonely fate

By another form of nakedness will be revealed

As his spirit seeks atonement in its earthly state.

He always knew he needed something in his misery

But this bare sight was not what he anticipated:

In the least of his brethren he had failed to see

That *there* would be the cornerstone a god created.

In the lust which long ago portended this affair

The seed of Nature lusted more for conscious truth

Than any dictates thrust on thinking apes to bear

By the artificial god they worshiped in his youth.

His simple youth could not conceive of powers greater

Than the heaven of a deity men called their own --

But who created such an upside-down creator

As would steal the very essence of his flesh and bone?

Nicodemus' lesson was a potent one indeed:

A teaching Jesus counseled for a struggling consciousness;

But it had to be another god who once decreed

The inner war men battled then in their duress...

Just as at life's turn he needed such a spirit-guide

To lift him from the lower form of instinct's course

Men advanced from beastliness to Nature's higher side

Through the love the prophet meant to tame that feral force.

But the mustard seed he then decreed was Nature's too --

What thing can grow but it be rooted in the ground?

And high upon the spirit-wind the seedling flew

Never yet since Adam's time to venture down.

The kingdom meant to grow from this analogy

Is the one within a man as Jesus said --

Not the fortress later men described to be

In the war proclaimed against the body by the head.

So thought grew great as Nature was degraded;

Hid within the body of an earthly beast

Whose thought a lovely banquet had created

But one the world must now declare a devil's feast.

Such ideas are hidden in the tales the ancients told --

But who relates their message to the modern soul?

The ego's version men must worship in their minds

While the deeper one yet functions by the old designs.

The god of thought is worshiped still and Nature pushed away

And remains the modern image men revere today.

But who conceives the modern idol they yet gape

Made their souls the victims of their own god's rape?

The Vision of the Rejected Prophet

A new form of the psyche's self-representation emerges, exposing the natural, unadorned reality of the unconscious: the animal foundations of our natures, expressed figuratively as nakedness. Jung wrote that nakedness is symbolic of the reality of the soul. The German philosopher, Friedrich Nietzsche, in a reference to the clergy, wrote: "I should like to see them naked; for, if they were truly men of god they would be ashamed to wear clothes." Nietzsche's intuitive mind penetrated the stark underside of a process which compensates dressed-up ego-images of who we think we are. Such re-interpretations of philosophical and religious ideas contribute to the ongoing dialectic between conscious and unconscious by elaborating the spiritual and psychological demands for a more personal and direct participation in the developmental changes confronting us today.

there gathered a multitude by the stream
and murmurings swelled through the crowd.
a prophet walked naked among them
and the people gasped at what they could not comprehend.
who among the throng could join themselves to the brazen man
who walked naked among them?
for they grieved at his nakedness and few could bear the tension
of the sight.
shouts rose amid the onlookers and jeers and insults rang from
the crowd:
what is this evil stirring now among us?
how is it we permit our eyes to fasten on this nakedness
startled though we are?
and surely their hearts were guilty.

and surely their guilt drove them from the place.

but there were several who remained.

they could not avert their eyes from the naked man and surely
they too were guilty.

the prophet spoke to them saying: how is it the guilty cannot
abide the sight of my nakedness but the truly afflicted?

yet even they but gape in disbelief?

do you not now feel your affliction?

and the afflicted few knew neither what they did nor why they
did as they gaped the nakedness of the man before them.

again the prophet spoke to them saying: would you be as apes?

despised by men?

and would you do as despised apes do?

one among the afflicted questioned the prophet saying:

would we know what we do?

while yet all men know not?

would we not weep openly at your nakedness while yet all men
weep alone in secret -- even from themselves?

thus are we afflicted.

surely your image has descended upon us;

for in the sufferings of our affliction we would know only of
apes and weeping.

and their buried souls flowed tears as they gaped the prophet
and their deformed bodies quivered at the sight.

once more the prophet exhorted them saying: do you feel the
power of the serpent who has invaded you?

the same serpent who was given before eden was even dreamt?

yet is there no woman among you who would entice you?

who is it then who has enticed you to your affliction?

one among the afflicted spoke saying: surely our souls have
been exposed to you.

indeed we burn with things we do not understand
for we have not the missing rib among us.

and the prophet answered thus: who among you would appease
the burden which has been placed upon you?

who among you would cultivate the painful command lodged
in your hearts?

who shall bear the guilt of the ape's body?

will you thus be driven to a ceaseless despair by the truths
conceived in you?

that the serpent of change has drawn the veil from your motives
and cast you into a darkness which you neither know nor
comprehend?

you were made from one and your own nature is rent from you.

you were made from one and nightly unto one are you returned.

you were made thus and each day are you horrified by the sight?

and the afflicted few gaped in horror and amazement at one
another;

and their distended bodies shook as they fixed on each
others' nakedness.

again the prophet spoke saying: nature it was who created
these needs in you.

the eternal night gave you this serpent who pre-existed eden.

nature's estranged spirit it was who tore the missing part from you
that the serpent would reveal the veil of your motives and it be
lifted from your afflicted eyes.

can you not now see what christ's wound opened?

that nature's spirit made this hole in you?

that your own small image is indiscernible from it?

that it could make you eat of the fruit but could not make you
comprehend the fig leaf?

strip you of your souls as you were made to act like animals

and you begged for it as if love had seized hold of your bodies?

but such things cannot abide but for little time --

for where do they go but into your hearts to work opposing forces?

you had strength to be shamed, embarrassed, and abased.

you grieved as you worshiped -- yet you had not strength to repent;

for how else could you feel such opposed forces so profoundly?

you were made to transgress the law though you feared it.

you were made to fear it that you would one day be humbled as
you transgressed it;

and now this day has come -- and you quake at the deed you've
done?

are you not thus humbled?

lower your eyes and slink away with false indignity like the others
if you cannot bear the sight...

how is it you stand there trembling, bound to the earth you
afflicted ones?

THE UNKNOWN WOMAN.

The distant psychic force has now become a living voice

Turning round the lofty notion he conceived as choice.

And the strange emotions it prescribes are drawing out

The Second Coming all the preachers talk about.

For centuries this long-awaited goal was trapped

In the lowest form the godly could conceive.

So enamored of their thought were they and so enrapt

Their own realities could not themselves believe.

But this should be forgiven for the problem isn't small;

Indeed it is the greatest one from times of old.

Its secret has been hidden in the darkest place of all --

The last retreat conceivable: the human soul.

This statement though should not be taken as facetious;

It leads to darker places than a man can know.

For every form of truth the mind conceives as specious

A greater mystery indeed lies far below...

So this man is driven to explore these darker places

Than just his meager criticisms have revealed;

And he is being urged to fill the empty spaces

In the gaps collective thinking has concealed.

THE ANCIENT KING.

The three-fold god of Christian thought shall yield before this task:

The reason he's so anxious now and deeply troubled.

For since he glimpsed the world beneath his philosophic mask

The secret nature of the paradox has doubled.

The language of its ancient truth is not discursive --

It tells a man's soul through the excrement of thought;

Its revelations always felt to be subversive

To the hallowed artificial culture men are taught.

It's the chief of the ways of God the book of Job described:

Nature's great Behemoth with its mighty bones of brass.

It's this ancient deity which now is circumscribed

That his individuality should come to pass.

Epistemology is flattered only by itself

As a world of Nature disappears behind its veil;

Sunk below the deep reflecting pool of Eden's stealth --

Confounded still by cloven hoof and horn and tail.

He fabled his grand thought had left such truths behind

But philosophy's enduring thought could not express

The strange intrusions in the background of his mind

The naked prophet now reveals in his undress;

Nor could science or theology avail such things

As men's collective knowledge for so long repressed

To spare themselves the labor of their wanderings

Through the darkness of their natures as their souls regressed.

What would this man's soul if it could speak reveal today?

Had it sinned against its function for a god deceived

To re-interpret its own savior in this mock display

Whose victims swore eons before they once believed?

His prophet speaks the longings of the thief then cast away

Whose nature was devoured by the dark unknown;

Risen now to light the beast who sent the light astray

And left him squatting with its burden all alone...

Such things collective thinking cannot apprehend --

They spring only from the lonely reaches deep within.

And all the king's horses and all the king's men

Can't put these two worlds back together again.

THE ODDLY SHAPED MAN.

Why am I so deeply shamed for being a man?

Save for my own inability to feel

The deeper reaches of my nature's dark demand

To form a formless god my thinking would conceal?

But for my troubled human heart to sole express

A god's redemption in the form of nakedness;

A nakedness the priests continue to defile

Since the day the fig leaf arbitrated style.

The leaf became a dress and their feminine shame

For the animal they hid beneath their god's acclaim.

A stranger to myself the Christian myth decrees

Though I have the body men despised for centuries.

It still laments the ruthless discipline incurred

By the fantasies inherited from distant creeds;

For its cries are not included in the Christian Word --

And the naked body has its own inherent needs.

Why guilt and shame should be so much associated

With a nature seeking to reveal to me my heart

Must be an even older testament than men created

To escape the darkness of the truth they split apart.

So opposed to Nature was their new reality

Mind and body split to form a strange morality;

And the guilt instilled by this Promethean offense

Must be in the body Nature formed for her intents.

I feel within my heart its god-likeness indeed --

Yet for all, a concept my small mind cannot concede.

THE UNKNOWN WOMAN.

This nakedness exposes what he's always been

That only now his inner nature will reveal:

For underneath the clothing of the thoughts of men

Lives an animal whose function is to feel.

The distorted forms these feelings have acquired

Garb the inner nature of the noblest soul;

And many outward things are then required

To clothe the emptiness of man's collective goal.

This goal has now commanded planetary scale

To escape the stark demands of inner space.

But the Mother Nature men endeavor to unveil

Also hides within their breasts her own neglected face:

A terrifying image to the universe of men

Who ever worship fantasies of Thought's desire;

Who've denied themselves and what they've always been

To don the sacred robes of heavenly attire.

The task this soul imposes is a weary one indeed --

It summons up the fear of guilt and pain and sin.

It suffers too the concrete gods of every distant creed

Projected on an outer world whose nature lies within.

THE ODDLY SHAPED MAN.

You know what? I'm tired of thoughts of gods and men;

But this urge still strives to clarify the shit I'm in.

Who birthed it? Why are some propelled so freely through it

And others laid to waste by what their minds intuit?

How can people be so different for all they share

When the same painful life attacks men everywhere?

And yet remain so much the same within their core

Even science can't explain away the gods we bore.

Are we driven to continue to conceal our shame

For an image we projected to reject what it disguised?

Still for all its hidden purposes in Jesus' name

For a power in us no man yet has recognized?

Has my objective striving only more confounded

The subjective nature at the root of my belief?

Has my scientific knowledge only now compounded

The secret pain from which I've so long sought relief?

Does the key of knowledge open yet another hold

Of a deeper wisdom from a strange elusive lock?

Or just another fantasy my frightened thought extolled

To stop the forward movement of the spirit's clock?

Have we dwarfed the heavens so with our collective pride

We forced the gods to pack their bags and steal aside?

Only now their holy dread to spread and scatter

Enthroned within the unknown properties of Matter?

THE ANCIENT KING.

Yet the *method* of science is the one chance he's got

To penetrate the mystery of this black dot...

The smallest speck of matter hides a mighty force

As the physicists revealed in their objective search --

A singular analogy for Nature's hidden course

Beneath the images exalted by the Christian Church.

The smallest speck of one man's soul reveals a world within:

One so it is stated only meekness shall inherit;

But one the Church revised anent the world of men --

Unwitting victims of their own demonic spirit.

What else could the prophet of the Western mind extol

To compensate the monsters who were destined to devour

Half the world and only pride themselves on what they stole

For little more than worldly wealth and greed and power?

Two thousand years of human fears and what have they achieved

But the very opposite for which their prophet grieved?

These two sides of this man's nature blindly disagree

Struggling on the cross of an old theology.

The two shadows hung upon his modern crucifixion

Are the two thieves judged in the Christian contradiction;

Whose ancient paradox is caught beneath the vanity

Of an ideal image meant to resurrect humanity.

As Christ was sent to suffer for its imperfections

He symbolized a god-like veil for its projections:

These incurred the lethal history beneath the love

Of a frightened Christian war with Nature from above...

Just as physics has a model for the facts it finds

This ancient myth reveals the model of the Western mind.

For centuries this model has described its worldly view

And like the model physics uses views an atom too:

The Adam of the earth-bound world religious thought reversed

When Nature's spirit-child denied the breast from which it nursed.

The spirit-child has grown to be a mighty little man

Who can split the force of Adams with his very hand.

But the fusion now resulting in the world of myth

Is Intellect and God this man is burdened with.

What once reached up to touch the sky in its desire

Now plunges down inside the lowly depths of matter.

Thus the man who once conceived a god as higher

Now a deeper darker deity must flatter.

One god cannot support a paradox alone --

For a paradox must presuppose a second thing.

While a new Jehovah has ascended to the throne

His vengeful side lies deep inside men's reckoning.

As Nature's force emerges from the dark unknown

Men again have proudly claimed creation as their own.

But the idol seeking power in the knowledge they have seized

Only by a god of equal strength may be appeased.

It resides in Nature as their intuition scents --

Though deeper symbols hide the myth she represents.

Who has yet seized power though but fleetingly employed

Was not himself by power in the end destroyed?

Whose god has not been rent apart by opposition?

Science sees but one though its history sees two;

Its purpose overpowered by a dark ambition

Now become the plaything of its own implicit view;

Yet directed by the only force it can't admit:

The spirit-power unimagined in the Thing

Which turned a prophet's mighty vision bit by bit

To little men who wanted love without the suffering.

In man's objective science and its ardent search for facts

The two opposing deities of worldly fate are found;

And as the mask of love concealed the older Church's acts

The scientific image too is upside-down...

In this man's re-vision of his model of perception

He must search the Janus-face of each opposing pair

To separate the power of his own deception

From the lovely garment Western thought pretends to wear.

The god of thought and Nature's law form two opposing sides:

The thought and feeling this man's now acquainted with;

But the counter-pole of her decree alone decides

The model for perception of his own small myth.

The great, the small -- the higher and the lower too --

All combine and separate to form his worldly view.

Nature shall arrange the pairs as only she can do --
The god-like burden is for him to follow through.

THE ODDLY SHAPED MAN.

I wrenched and cried for these ideas and knew not why.
Who thinks what every fiber of his culture must deny?
Am I the scapegoat of a spirit for its own sacrifice
To an unimpeded power which itself cannot suffice?
Whose darkness has arranged the world in such a morbid way
Its only goal in Life is only life's decay?
Whose awareness of its majesty through men had poured
Only then for all their painful trials to be ignored?
Did God himself not sacrifice his own begotten son
That he should feel the guilt and suffering of Nature's loss?
When from her Eden he expelled the older sinful one
Who forced his own atonement too upon that painful cross?
How is it my dark vision once described the cross as bare
As still and silent I sat smoking on my little throne?
Yet squatting with the burden Nature forced on me to bear
For myself and gods as well her power to atone.

THE DARK PRINCE.

What would Adam say to God if asked today
The progress of this gift of consciousness to tell?
That it subdued the outer world in every way
Though in the inner one did not quite work so well?
The winding course of history has wound about --
Just as in his little world, also in the great --
The mythic force caught deep inside and can't get out

But through the little fantasies his thoughts relate...

Here he needs the concepts he worked hard to understand

To find his bearings in this archetypal sea.

The two thieves vying for the soul of this small man

Personify the natural dichotomy

Crucifying his own passion for his former life

To prepare the god of consciousness' identity

For the archetype of mid-life labor's sacrifice.

These are the opposites beneath the dark disguise

Of the concepts ancient men once formulated

Through the value-judgments Jesus came to symbolize:

The fate of conscious pride their partial thought created.

The elemental forces which reflect themselves

In the sacred stories men have always treasured

Expose the hidden forms behind subjective veils

Of objective truths by which each man is measured.

The higher sphere of god-like Thought's existence

Confounding still the secret one of Nature's urge

Creates the agonizing drama of resistance

For her force to tear apart his modern demiurge.

His little life is not so very far removed

From those who suffered in the past this world's insistence:

That history should doubt what science thought it proved

And begin to form a new myth in the distance.

The dark seed of sickness this man's struggling with --

The rejected healing power in his own soul --

Is the round-about creation of his own small myth

Urging him with fantasies of being whole.

Without these contradictions where would he have been

In this crazy backward world of gods and men?

Threading dreams together one step at a time

By exposing the projections of the conscious mind.

He may never know the purposes it chases

As he stumbles through the darkness of his wretched soul;

But he may feel the wonder of these magic places

And the deeper mysteries they silently unfold

If he connects the history his thought embraces

To the reasons why little soul was sold...

The Alchemical Serpent

Many ancient cultures, including early Christian Gnostics, considered the serpent as a deity: a symbol of transformation and nature's wisdom. With the growing establishment of orthodox Christianity, a vulnerable consciousness, yet driven toward a separate identity, repressed the nature-symbol and became hostile to the unconscious and its dark, earthly reality. The modern appearance of the snake in dreams symbolizes the influence of this deeper animal wisdom, often felt as poisonous by the conscious mind because of its estrangement from the natural world. The ancient symbol of the uroboros – the serpent with its tail in its mouth – reflects the "self-fertilizing" process which later evolved into the symbol of Communion: the eating of Christ's body and the drinking of his blood, a psychic analogy of digesting and assimilating the spirit-world of one's own unconscious nature.

THE ANCIENT KING.

> This rejected healing power is the older snake:
> The ancient guardian of Nature's transformation;
> Its forked tongue describing two directions when it spake
> To its chthonic partner luring Adam to temptation.
> Poor Adam! Tricked unaware to seek a double-life
> Yet to toil like a common beast upon the earth;
> Deceived not only by his nature but his own wife --
> From his own rib was this deception brought to birth!
> If this were not enough for one small man to ponder
> An even greater task upon poor Adam fell:
> For though the fate of Eden found him soon to wander
> It informed him in the deed he was a god as well!
> Just a little one it's true but mighty nonetheless --

Certainly enough to overpower snakes and Eves.

Even little gods are not required to confess

To such lowly creatures as the dust of earth conceives.

There was just the one small matter of the guilt he bore

And for centuries this god-like burden plagued his mind.

But the little god in him repressed it more and more

That an easier and nicer Lord might be divined.

So tolerant was this new god to the world of men

He relieved them every one of all their guilt and sin;

Immortal life bequeathed them too for a job well-done

In the wise rule of earth's affairs in their dominion.

Despite their smart command and the good faith they worked

The unfathomed God of Darkness in their hearts still lurked.

They tried to make it go away but it scarce would leave --

Still the new Lord told them they had only to believe.

They sacrificed a scapegoat to this New Testament

And convinced themselves the more their truth was heaven-sent.

But the God of Darkness was not easily appeased;

Its truth was *not* the one men fashioned in the Word.

On the very heel of the deepest plea it seized

And by order of the older god remained unstirred...

Had they looked inside the centuries of their despair

They'd have seen this ancient serpent-god's primeval gaze.

But Nature's symbol was condemned in the old affair

For an image more inclined to flattery and praise.

As if the laws of Nature cared if they were censured

By a little god whose worship of his own pride

Thought if only he believed enough he would be cured

Of the task this serpent symboled on the inside.

Tail in mouth it formed the circle of a process

That wed, consumed, and slayed itself and then gave birth

To the otherworldly god of human consciousness

Whose naked little body never left the earth.

THE UNKNOWN WOMAN.

This transforming power was repressed and vilified

In an ancient myth designed to serve the pride of man;

And a frightened lonely beast itself identified

With the very power it could never understand.

What Jesus suffered to atone this mighty sin

Through the god-forsaken trials of Nature's urge

Was a symbol of the spirit of the self within

To allow the truth of *inner* nature to emerge:

His suffering analogized the sacrifice

Of a human animal whose faith accepted

The fate of powers far beyond its own small life --

A task the vanity of consciousness rejected.

This god-man's fate was a reflection of the state

Of future forms in consciousness' evolving quest

That man's unconscious seized for him to contemplate

The dark opposing forces in his own small breast.

This is what the demons of possession are about --

The starkest testaments embodied in the most devout:

The old god of a frightened beast who feared its own growth

Indulging only half a truth whose myth contains them both.

To examine its own soul would truly be too much

For then it might discover how its priests were out of touch

With their own redemption and their fathers' Holy Ghost

At which the frightened beast could look -- but not too close.

So their truth became the frenzy of their own allure

Possessed by bright delusions of a god's grandeur;

And the fantasies their souls were forced to compensate

Made the great become the little and the little great.

THE DARK PRINCE.

This man still feigns a vein of pride in what he thinks about

Though a prudent man must ponder what his pride reveals;

For the true companion of man's honesty is doubt

And the truth is often caught in what his pride conceals.

If a man's pride indeed goeth before a fall

It's a wonder this man has any left at all.

But the true companion of a man's pride is fear:

The *real* god demanding tribute from a life down here.

Deep inside men's faith and knowledge this god lays its snare --

All men's certainty reveals its power everywhere.

This truth has led this man inside the cloud of Time

When ancient men were frightened by the force they fought;

Quite like the modern ones who shrink before the crime

Of re-inspecting contradictions ancient fathers taught.

But evolution yet insists the minds of men address

The painful split the Western ego has created;

For, the double meaning Nature's opposites express

Must find this ego's mythic tale to be outdated.

The inner man still strives to advertize projections

Of such images as symbols of the mind's extremes;

Yet a deeper effort must interpret such reflections

Than to worship idols fashioned by his conscious dreams.

This deeper effort leads to more than flat rejection

Of the ancient truths concealed within the modern mind.

Science too is guilty in the opposite direction

Of the certain pride to which the preacher is confined.

Still striving in the outside world against the fear

Of the inner terms concealed in its prospectus

It denies that any form of knowledge could appear

In the modern soul of Homo Intellectus.

THE ODDLY SHAPED MAN.

We now are what a distant ego dreamed we'd be:

Marvels who perform our miracles collectively;

Raised mighty works in a world once dark and grave

Where once we kindled fire in a prehistoric cave.

We were young, half-dozing, clinging frightened to the pack;

Animal creations and when threatened we thought back

In a battle for survival as in all instinctive brutes

Competing in a world where only violence yields its fruits;

Needing only to pursue the gift of our volition

With the fragile spark an unknown god imagined in us

To bear the magic apple of its own cognition

In a beast as strong in packs as alone was tenuous.

The distant god of consciousness required sacrifice

On the spirit-fires of beastly images to guide;

And the magic animal was then reflected twice:

In the god his thought would be and the beast his thought denied.

Indeed today we sacrifice the Nature-world within

To the image of the little gods our thoughts would be;

Yet frightened in a huddle in the cave we still are in --

The forbidden fruit enticing from the same opposing tree.

Though we're threatened more today by perils we can't see

And Nature's cave has since become the dark analogy

Of a frightened human struggle in its twice-reflected quest

To reproduce the consciousness its consciousness repressed.

Is this the god who made me in the image of its own?

Bequeathed to me a painful world and left me all alone

With but the quiet whisper in the stillness of my soul

For Nature to inform me of a dark and distant goal?

Which through the course of history is only half-revealed

To a human brute whose image of its soul concealed?

Whose likeness is the image I am fashioned in:

The image Nature gave me or the idol I pretend?

Who struggles on the cross of *that* unconscious night?

Which opposing image is the nature I now fight?

THE UNKNOWN WOMAN.

He finds himself sunk deep in this forbidden cave

Long ago compelling him toward the fruit it gave:

The spirit's big-bang blast which in his youth had hurled

His unwitting consciousness before the spirit-world;

Where Nature's truth flashed deeper facts before his eyes

To prepare him for a life no thought could compromise.

For, the paradox his hidden soul related

Was the one the human spirit inculcated;

Only later to reveal through his conflicted youth

The dark enigma of its contradicting truth.

Its reality is not the one he once conceived

Nor yet is it the image modern minds revere;

Always had it changed its shape when he believed

His partial consciousness had made its image clear.

But what religious history has proved at least --

Despite the contradicting statements of its past --

Is that a god is yet entangled with a beast;

That a man will find himself between the two at last

Ascending to the god his conscious pride thought clear

Yet fleeing from the animal he left behind in fear.

Though both combine to underline the conscious fiction

Of a frightened mythic flight from Nature's contradiction

For an unacknowledged opposite yet half-conceived

By a half-Christian man who only half-believed.

THE DARK PRINCE.

The contradiction now begins to take *real* form –

The reason he's so oddly shaped indeed;

For it wrenched his conscious mind outside the norm

To seek the monstrous nature of its own need.

It was a serpent so great it swallowed him whole.

He fought in it for years with the little tools he had

Doing weak-kneed penance for the ancient fruit he stole

In a world who worships such ideas yet deems them mad.

This same great serpent lodged itself in Nietzsche's mouth –

The very opposite of Jonah's tale inside the whale;

For Nietzsche's own thinking turned the image inside-out

In pretense as the king of his subjective tale.

He rejected all the subtle truths between the lies

That could have brought his intuitions back to earth;

As he laughed insanely in his heavenly disguise

And spit the serpent out before it brought to birth

The earthly spirit it was meant to fertilize.

His deeds then exemplified the same Christian story

Describing human supermen in all their glory;

To lure him to the madness of the depths he breached

And turn away the light for which his spirit reached...

But he sketched out a warning for the Supermen

Whose egos form a shield from the abyss:

For, all the madness Nietzsche's mind had borne within

Still overtook his country nonetheless.

THE ANCIENT KING.

This force strikes fear and awe in a man's heart --

For in its strength it tears whole worlds apart.

Job saw the vision just as Nietzsche did;

As countless others in the ruthless march of Time.

And each was humbled by the mighty force he hid

Beneath the cloak of culture in his conscious mind...

This man is humbled too, quite like those other men;

This has gained him energy to undertake his sin.

And facing sin's a crime too as he soon shall see

When his burden cracks the shell of fear and vanity.

But he still relates such things to pride's feeble gaze --

Nature's truth deflected yet by thought's reflecting glaze;

Still harbors secret flights within his earth-bound soul --

Fancies he can tame the beast who threats to make him whole.

But humility turned upside-down humiliates;

He must search his soul with care what for his pride creates.

For hidden in the fantasies of his projection

Lies the naked creature of his own self-rejection...

His expectations though must suffer some delay --

Only Time and effort seed the spirit's oracle;

Even more so for the modern cast of thought today

Whose inner life is little but rhetorical.

This man has pierced the veil of sense perception's guise

Though concrete elements invade his thinking still:

This most basic feature of the modern mind belies

A form of thought where only objects can be real.

Only when the image of these objects is perceived

Can it be broken down to yield the soul's projections;

A fearful burden for the man in him who once believed

His small thought could somehow master such reflections...

Thus to thread illusions is a slippery affair:

A man may think he's reached the peak a thousand times;

Only to discover with exhaustion and despair

A range of mountains far beyond the little hill he climbs.

THE DARK PRINCE.

He now knows what Mephistopheles to Faust once said

As Goethe fought these mythic figures in his head:

"Here where we stand the steps are steeper.

You grapple with a realm most strange

And wantonly would plunge in debt still deeper."

This was when his worldly soul began to change

As he faced the psychic background of the land of dreams:

The misty scene of Nature's looming mountain range:

A world whose mystery is never what it seems...

The identity of this man soon will be replaced

By the same collective deities he fought before;

Only now the little mantle which he then embraced

Reveals a world of Instinct through its mythic lore;

Where compulsive laws determine what a man believes

Behind the grand and regal garment of Appearance;

Far beyond the ten commandments of the moral thieves

Whose buried souls seek upside-down adherence.

His nature now demands these specters be discerned

Amid the blinding images enrobing their deceit;

For, the spirit-fire the depths of men have ever burned

Lies within the inner core of earth beneath their feet.

It beams its symbols through the light their consciousness emits

At the same time reflecting back the consciousness it shaped.

It guards the ancient throne on which the Unknown sits

To hide from fools the deeper truths they only aped.

The mantles and the guarding, the specters and the throne

Are only vague descriptions of this dark unknown --

The strange abyss through which a consciousness is thrown:

The cosmic world beyond the god he called his own...

THE UNKNOWN WOMAN.

This cosmic world hides many other things as well

Beyond the myth of lofty kingdoms and the gates of Hell.

Like the Hydra standing sentry at those bolted gates

A changing myth conceals more things than it relates.

When from its many heads a single truth is shorn

Two more upon its fearsome shoulders then are born.

That any man should not adjudge himself too wise:

The paradox is doubled when an old myth dies.

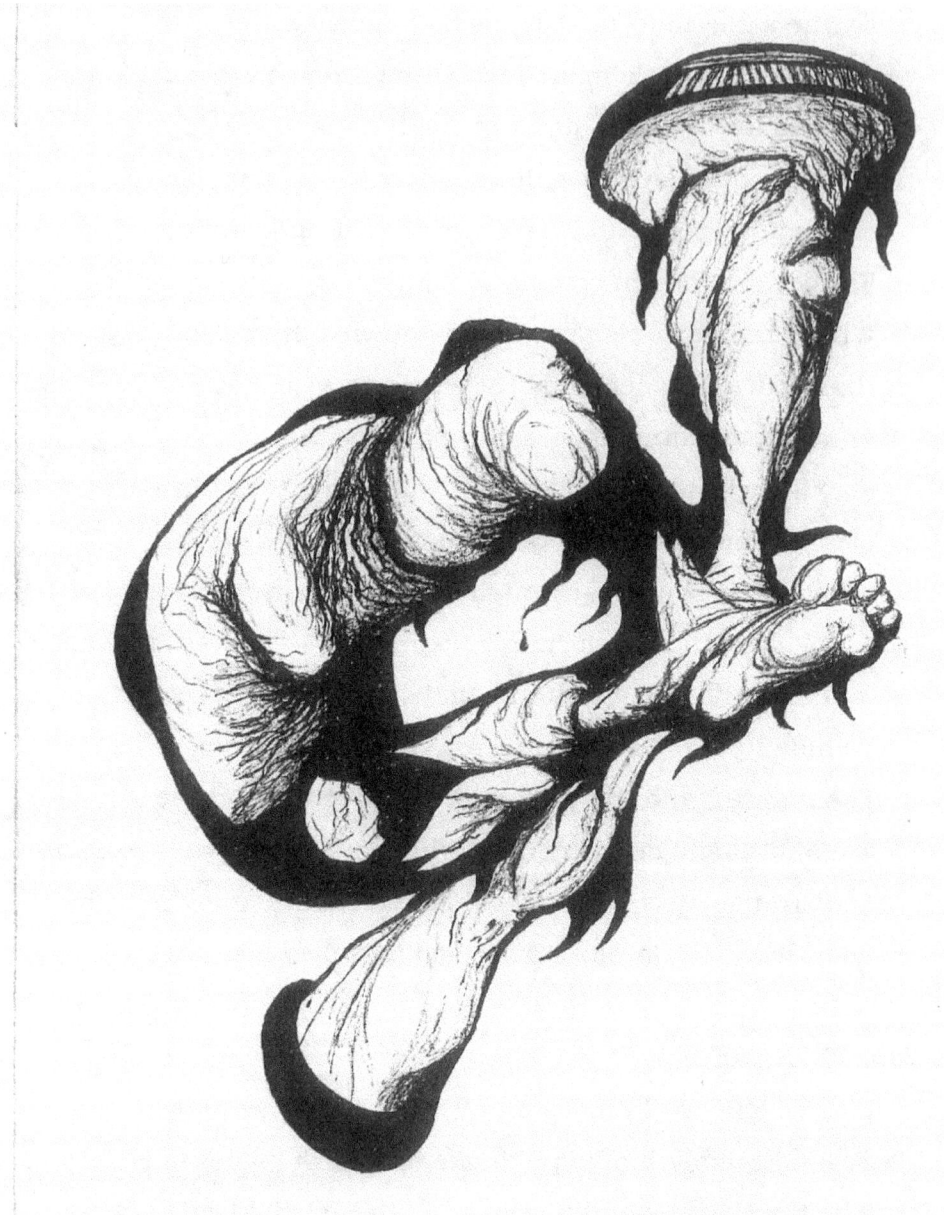

When consciousness descends from outer space
To separate the deeper conflicts down below
The creative fight in this forbidden place
Will find him in the depths -- his own black dot to know.

His soul is changing too for functions once neglected;

For in the fiery depths new life is in the making

To compensate the little god he once protected

From the greater one whose force is slowly waking.

The functions this old mythic model symbolized

Are tools of life created by the Dark Unknown

For purposes his consciousness had long surmised

Were only for itself and for itself alone;

A childish adaptation consciousness must hide

As his spirit seeks to put such childish things aside.

And yet for every truth this spirit vindicates

Another paradox of truth it soon creates...

THE DARK PRINCE.

His little god personifies his modern point of view

From the vantage point of ancient powers far below;

And the compensations for the little world he thought he knew

Must dissolve before this universe he seeks to know:

The spirit-breath within the soul of Adam Nature blew

That birthed a man whose Word a greater wind would blow

Than any of the plagues of death Jehovah's anger threw

At the men whose idols still are gods they can't let go.

To become again the sacred children Christ alluded to

Men must re-experience a world from long ago:

The simple undivided one from which their natures grew --

Too complicated by the fruit they stole for them to know.

How a man must struggle through the follies of his youth

Only to refute them in the guise of his ascent!

Could ever youthful follies have concealed the seeds of truth?

Could history be circular? Is that what Jesus meant?

Reflection is the fruit of Nature man was meant to use;

How much life remains concealed beneath the past's disguise?

The shadow-acts of history are easy to excuse

Yet only through reflection of the past can men be wise.

If ancient men analogize the child of man today

What strange emotions represent this childhood state?

What mysteries have modern idols swept away

Whose living values only Nature can create?

The little god is gone who formed his bailiwick --

One more step in a lengthy process filled with doubt.

Though Christ with just a word or touch could heal the sick

It takes many fitful years to get *this* demon out.

At the base of such a task is a stark reality --

Not the myth in which a man may suddenly be healed.

This older power turning round his personality

Only through the most devoted effort is revealed...

So he must be smaller still to squeeze through the little door

That once awakened Alice to the wonderland she saw;

But it's no child's fairytale he's bidden to explore

And he knows well the black and frightful side of Instinct's law.

This law lies hidden in compulsion -- all are subject to it;

Whether Good or Bad is in their minds and how they view it.

For, the self-reflection mirrored in the conscious light

Must beam its own image back inside a guarded night.

This reveals the function in which man, like God, was made:

The image of the bargained soul for which the Devil paid.

In this bargain both must yield and sacrifice;

For any two who forge a pact both must pay a price.

This process binds each over to a higher fate --

A bond now presenting him the ancient narrow gate.

But he must be careful not to puff himself too high;

Only lately has its vision dawned before his eye.

This crime he commits is not a thing to sell or buy

And he must hold his devil tight to know the reasons why.

THE ODDLY SHAPED MAN.

Should I trust my own eyes? My sore afflicted eyes?

That once could not judge properly an object's shape or size?

The Janus-faced figures I then squinted through the mist

All the strange alluring women in my dreams I kissed;

The nameless wraiths intruding on my sleeping mind --

The fleeting ghosts who when I turned around were gone;

The night-time harbingers I crawled through filth to find

To shine the faintest light of consciousness upon...

The visions which awakened me and made my heart to race;

Have they really etched this erring crooked path I face?

The nights I shook in bed and started at the slightest sound

The tension bound around me, found me kneeling on the ground;

The despised and ugly visage of the heavy toad I've crowned:

Are these the real foundations of the backward faith I found?

THE ANCIENT KING.

He shall do well to keep such lowly things in sight;

For, the spirit his unwitting thought imbibed

Shall only show its shadow-face at night

And it must be more thoroughly described

To bring its wondrous ways before the light...

He has not exposed himself -- naked though he stands;

For his littleness has not yet been accepted

By the darker power who created these demands

That the image of his soul be resurrected.

He's worked hard thus far to keep his flame tindered

Against the ancient spirit-wind that swept him down.

And he shall need the strength this labor has engendered

To keep his thinking firmly rooted to the ground.

This force has seen the course of many lured astray

For thinking they beheld the light of prophecy.

The mid-point place where lambs and lions seek to lay

Is as double-faced as any other fantasy.

If he's learned nothing else he's learned this painful fact --

And it lies at the heart of the cognitive act.

THE ODDLY SHAPED MAN.

It must be the nature of a strange psychology

Mocking daily the accomplishments I labor for.

For, all I've done it seems I've done unconsciously

And each step forward takes me backward three or four.

The pain of these regressions through my double-mind

Leaves me even more distraught than when I first began

To seek these hazy images still half-defined

Hid behind the doorway to this magic land.

One day sees a light but dimly glowing

Soon shrouded by a moonless night as dark and vast

As any in this process yet bestowing

Since first I had consumed love's sweet repast.

The two-way mirror of my dreams is upside-down;

Its glass it seems reflects me everywhere.

The image only yesterday I swore I found

Now leers out at me through every passing stare.

The stranger things I see behind the grinning faces

Surely are the phantoms of my own distress:

The soul-sickness of a dark obscure crisis

And a thing which other souls need not confess.

So I turn inward and forsake the grinning faces

As I cross my legs and light another cigarette

For a smog of smoke to fill the empty spaces

A squandered soul endeavors daily to forget.

I've found no meaning yet in all the empty grins --

In all the squandered souls and their forgotten sins.

The soul's affliction, only, resurrects the dead

And compensates the myth the Christian mind has spread...

But this image I've ingested is leavened indeed --

It ferments within my heart a terrifying creed:

A dark and unknown me pretending it is grinning

To face the background of a fairytale beginning.

Are these just my thoughts, my fears, my own contradiction?

The leavened bread of my sick soul? My own affliction?

THE UNKNOWN WOMAN.

Here indeed his modern head will benefit

From the ancient sea in his unconscious mind.

For, the unexplored emotions being rent from it

Will soon elaborate the burden they assigned.

They form his thoughts as they conform in all men too;

They seek a depth below the Christian brand of sinning

A deeper well than he imagined lies in store
Than the fairytales the Christian world prepared him for.
The earthly force beneath this ritual protection
Finally will show itself through its reflection.

To shape a greater and more comprehensive view

Of the shadow-facts these images are spinning.

Slowly are they drawing his afflicted nature through

The smaller fantasy of his projected grinning...

This contradiction only Nature can unlock

Just as she reversed the movement on the Spirit's clock:

A stature small enough to fit this narrow door

Yet reflections wider than they ever were before.

THE DARK PRINCE.

Already he's descending once again;

If indeed he ever yet ascended

From the matrix of this universe within

Whose reality through fantasy portended

He would answer the philosophy of ancient men.

For his nature's needs were not quite satisfied

With the myth imposed on him from long ago;

And very foreign circumstances now decide

The changing myth emerging from below.

If he were the little god he used to be

He'd pull another answer from his hat;

Dismiss it all as useless morbid fantasy

And his little intellect would be content with that.

But his affliction found him seeking far beyond

The trappings of Appearance in his modern time;

For his intellect could not create the bond

To heal the split in his unconscious mind.

For fantasy forever was and always is

The secret meant to mediate the opposites in man.

It points beneath the level of appearances
To Creation and its enigmatic plan...
These creative powers now release their stream
In the little man who struggles on with all his might
To understand the inner man whose ancient dream
Seeks to be acknowledged by the Christian light.

THE ODDLY SHAPED MAN.

I feel the mythic wonder of the child I once knew
Spread beneath the comfort of his little twin bed:
A world of fantasy grown men are not accustomed to --
The timeless mist from which my manly spirit fled;
Charged with the excitement of a child's ecstatic view
Of the magic land of Fantasy within my head.
The little door is opening and symbols flood my mind
With amniotic images from Nature's silent womb;
Revealing shadows of the secret purpose she designed
To re-create the squandered soul she once consumed.
I see Pinocchio the little wooden toy
Whom old Geppetto crafted from a solid block.
He yearns today to be a real live little boy
And not the wooden puppet other children mock.
A Faustian homunculus now hovers near
Enclosed within the bubble of a human tear.
My grandmother whispers in a ghostly flowing gown
Who says she loves me as she smiles and gazes down;
The god who with his own teeth tore his flesh in sacrifice
In Zosimos' vision of the underside of Christ.
Just like the older serpent who consumed his own tail

The alchemists gave human form to Nature's dark travail:

A glimpse inside the depth of life profound and horrifying

Yet Nature's own expression of the living form of dying.

I see the ancient Ra whose agéd body twitched with death

From the serpent Isis kneaded from his drooling breath.

I feel the shadows of a universe of odd-shaped men

Whose natures sought to crown them through their guilt and sin.

The naked prophet rises eerily before me;

The thronging multitude is gathered by the stream.

In them, childhood's shadows in the twilight forming

The pain of memories returning in my waking dream.

I watch the march of ancient armies mobilized for war

Steeled in readiness for feuds their histories created --

Who suddenly forget what they are fighting for

As modern minds for new realities are fated.

I see wine bibbers, prostitutes, and thieves

Received within the welcoming embraces

Of the Spirit and the wayward course it weaves

To scatter light upon their weary faces.

I feel the frightened pleas of Love in the abyss

The gentle touch of painful years, the softness of its kiss.

I see the great beast's torment in his sad and piercing eyes

Forming once the guilt and self-defeat of my demise.

The fruit of hubris crowning once the tree of righteousness

Has fallen down inside the ground of a dark abyss.

As Nebuchadnezzar's dream unveiled his kingly fate

Men must suffer still these perils from an ancient date.

Where once a mighty tree had spread its branches out

Daniel resurrects the smaller seed of Nature's sprout.

Yet I fear the strange anxiety such dreams induce

For the years of struggle buried in what they produced.

I fear my own mind and the life in me created

By the underworldly things on which I concentrated.

I fear the inner spirit-god who put me through all this;

I once feared my misery -- I now fear consciousness...

The Design of Christian Dogma

Christian dogma allows the individual to participate in the divine drama within the safety of collective containment. Group identification serves as an instinctive defense mechanism designed to protect a vulnerable ego from the direct experience of unconscious demands: the "fall into the hands of the living God" and its often frightening and over-powering opposition. Theology was a product of careful deliberation on the gradual accrual of unconscious energy to the images and ideas attracting and directing its attention. In the early course of development, a fragile ego identified only with the ideal side of conscious desire. Historically, for the purpose of strengthening consciousness, the dark side of the unconscious regulating function was repressed. The introverted nature of religious devotion in the past enabled it to operate unconsciously. The changing conditions of development today, however -- the anxiety driving the current swing toward extraversion – are beginning to push this repressed side into consciousness. Its acceptance as an inner conflict opens the door to the emotional/spiritual energy that lies beneath the self-flattery and certainty needed to support an earlier stage of consciousness.

THE DARK PRINCE.

>These deceptive fantasies will sweep him off his feet
>For Nature's secrets when revealed will do just that.
>But from his mouth too will tear the bitter witch's teat
>Once nourishing the blinded bitterness he spat...
>Though for now the superstitions in this childhood land
>Represent the fear of his inherited belief:
>The uninspected part of him who jeered the naked man

Whose zeal had underestimated this rejected thief.

The gods of history impose exceeding tension

On those who venture to oppose their dark decrees;

Compelled in ways beyond their human apprehension

By those very gods whose opposites they must appease.

In this twilight realm he feels afraid and rightly so;

These images are perilous for grown-up men.

They possess the mind with such a fascinating glow

Only fear can compensate the fantasies they spin.

They lead to pride the siren bride of all discovery.

Fear is his protection from this all-too-human trait;

For, nursing on the bitter witch's teat of misery

Alone reveals the truths these gods endeavor to re-state.

But he needs refuge from the fear such needs instill:

The flip-side of the siren bride this task imposes.

Far beneath his fantasies is something very real --

An aspect the collective violently opposes.

The fear of this offense has long since gripped his being

For the children born of history were grown men too

Whose sufferings once formed the fantasies he's seeing

From the terrors their realities compelled them through.

These fantasies combine at once *two* forces in his mind:

The compensations needed on his little twin bed

To protect him from the ancient thieves who lurk behind

The modern mythic battle being waged inside his head.

He's unaccustomed to their dark cooperation --

He's worked for years for it with everything he's got;

Only now when it reveals its secret operation

He's so frightened of its spectral task he sees it not.

Though half-aware of its convulsive after-shocks
A great tectonic movement formed this wave of symbol;
And the energy this world of mystery unlocks
In its wake leaves gods and men alike to tremble.
This paralyzing fear can turn a god to stone
As men's beliefs have testified for centuries.
Yet embedded in these idols Nature labors on
Enticing men to penetrate her mysteries.

THE ODDLY SHAPED MAN.

They seemed like clouds around a thinking lost in time
Imagining the mystery beneath the Word.
I never knew such mysteries with words could rhyme --
To my former rationality it seemed absurd.
But the Word *was* God or so the ancient ones declared
And though a small one it provided me the link
To the spirit-world my nature had prepared
To balance what it seeks with what I think.
The world of feeling to the scientific mind
Is the hostile brother of the literal domain.
It leads inside the spirit-world concealed behind
The real apparent one the scientists explain.
Just as alchemy pursued its spirit in the stone
Modern science seeks its answers in a world of sense;
Though now in its obsession with the concrete world alone
Has sacrificed the spirit at the soul's expense.
The world of alchemy was doubled when projected.
The intellect had not then scaled Olympus' height;
And beneath the modern edifice its truth erected

Its cornerstone lies buried now and out of sight.

The concrete sphere of visible reality

Still enchains the worldly spirit in its grasp.

Like Copernicus I view the inner galaxy

Compelling now my earthly consciousness to ask:

Whether round its globe indeed a universe rotated

Or was not a smaller one this universe created?

And whether like Columbus sailing half-way round the map

Nature also proved the inner world no longer flat?

THE UNKNOWN WOMAN.

These symbols weave around his thoughts in dark array

To help his consciousness establish where he is.

And he must concentrate on what they have to say

For he is being driven to this squandered soul of his.

The images informing him are things unique;

Aspects his unconscious mind has carefully prepared:

The flower of its own growth through centuries to seek

The magic image his collective thought impaired.

This is his affliction -- how he sees it is important;

For the causal view of consciousness remains unsquared

And the fleeting underside of it is most discordant

To the surface axioms the intellect declared.

Its structure is dissolved within the sphere below it

As a world of fantasy becomes experience;

And in the efforts he has made to come to know it

He may soon achieve his own unique deliverance...

THE DARK PRINCE.

The labor for the symbol that would heal the split

Requires consciousness to shine its light on it;

For, what is the value of a thing created

If its purposes cannot be clearly stated?

He may be struck a thousand times by passion's dart --

A thousand times may feel its wound within his heart;

But if he doesn't in the end perceive its goal

A thousand more he yet must suffer in his soul.

What is the value of the art such souls produce

If its significance cannot be put to conscious use?

Doubtless it relieves the artist and the patron too

Of the labor of its meaning in a man's subjective view.

It may, as well, relieve a certain pressure on his brain --

Maybe just enough to keep from feeling he's insane.

But when a man is working in the labor of his soul

Any notions of insanity go straight to hell.

Nature only births a diamond from a lump of coal

Where the dark beliefs of other men have ceased to dwell.

There will be no patron then to help him understand:

This outside referent is not his truth to tell.

And he must push himself beyond its countermand

To liberate a newborn function from its spell.

His nature now prepares to birth a living thing

But only in collaboration with it will he learn:

The spectral treasures Nature's inner world may bring

Only round the ceaseless wheels of opposition turn.

This requires too the application of his wit

But only in the service of the symbols bound to it.

The masculine identity of thought must come to own

That in truth a goddess always sat upon its throne.

THE ANCIENT KING.

As good and evil represent it in the Western mind

This Deity perceived by thought is only half-divined.

Indeed the mind reflects itself in such a way

To circumscribe the force that in its own depths lay.

But it reveals too the mind's relation to this force --

The unconscious aspects caught in these reflections.

These provide a man with symbols of the hidden course

Of his nature's evolution through the soul's projections.

Just as in a smaller thing a greater truth may hide

The self-aversion this man long has struggled with

Reflects the very images once trapped inside

The paradox of guilt and sin in the Christian myth.

The thought he once conceived was far above such things

Only found him deeper in the Valley of the Kings

Amid the stone-hewn tributes of an ancient race

To a god-like animal his thought could not replace.

He could not conceive the depth his guilt provided

And just as in the Christian myth remained divided

Until his misery created in his own black hole

The depth in him required to perceive his soul.

Men long have knelt in prayer to a god who sent his son

For Adam's sin to suffer for ignoring his command.

But consciousness became the sin of Eden's favored one

And the conscious suffering of law became the fate of man...

But there still remains a mythic labor to be done

Before these two distinguished worlds are sensed as one.

There yet are contradictions he can't speak about

Until his own nature fetches deeper riddles out.

THE ODDLY SHAPED MAN.

I hear the pleas of memories from years ago

When first I'd seen the stranger dream my life had been:

Not only that an anxious dread I couldn't know

Had slowly stolen my direction from within

But the gradual awareness it was always so

When I processed all the dreams I dreamt back then.

Through those years I watched as all my happy friends

Collapsed beneath the weight of my projections;

And lonely grimaces replaced the outward grins

As human scarecrows hurried off in all directions.

Few survived that great and terrible ordeal;

Few remained to lend their warm affections.

But the few who did revealed a face so real

Not hell itself could sever their connections.

Though unwittingly I tried in my obsessions

To drive them from my sore fragmented life;

And though I ended up with few possessions

The hearts I knew reserved such loving sacrifice

I owe them kinder forms of my confessions

Than the ones throughout my misery I told --

I must thank them from my heart for their concessions

When I lent to them the perils of my soul.

For love gazed back at me through my depressions

From one who listened to the crazy things I said;

And she patiently reflected my regressions

To provide me solid ground beneath my tread.

And even though she didn't always understand

The strange compulsions of an oddly driven man

She shone inside my black retreat the light of her relief

From the all-consuming darkness of my nature's grief.

THE DARK PRINCE.

What always was superfluous is burned away

By the Spirit's fire rekindled in his heart;

And hidden in the ashes now his essence lay

As the phantoms of his former world must now depart.

Soon a new-birthed life will wrench its way out of the ground:

The first formations of a human being in the round...

THE UNKNOWN WOMAN.

Once again emotions are a more instructive guide

Than the intellect and its interrogation light;

For the most important things in life may often hide

Beneath a man's abstractions in the plainest sight.

The two opposing gods he worked to reconcile

By a conscious act have now split into four;

And nothing could anticipate in grander style

The dark perplexities his logic must endure.

No more is he in debt to lords of the collective:

The opposites inherent in the psyche's imagery.

The smaller life he has endured has gained perspective

Of the little pair conceived beneath his misery.

When he tore away the magic mantle of the Devil

His feeling side the lofty god of thought revealed;

And when he pierced the darkness of this deeper level

Compelled the Shining One his female side to yield.

For, the opposites the Tree of Knowledge brought to birth

Are often dressed as male and female here on earth.

Thus the symbols turn around their own opposing pole

To expose the earthly nature of his Christian soul.

THE ANCIENT KING.

It's a fact: the deeper part of his internal world

Gravitated round the image of a little girl.

For what was veiled was what the naked prophet meant

In the vision of affliction and the missing rib he sent.

This is how the soul of one small man may come to birth

And grasp the female aspect of the deity on earth.

So the Father, the Son, and the shrouded Holy Ghost

Must suffer pagan guests in their patristic sphere;

For they contain the dark the light requires most:

The earthly goddess and the beast of Nature now appear

From behind the blood-red cloak the Devil held so close.

Scant wonder dogma failed the heaven he once sought:

Without the world of Nature there is no creative thought.

The ground of being Christian dogma strove to quell

Became the starkest mirror mythic tales could ever tell.

THE DARK PRINCE.

The patriarchal sphere the Trinity once gated

Is under siege by what his nature re-created:

The little girl now stands in stark contrast

To the masculinity of revelations past.

She soon will pave the way for reconciliation

With the dark objective power of a new revelation.

It was the task embedded in the dream long ago --

The nature he once dreaded and could not have guessed:

The Voice who told him all these years it must be so –

The opposite his masculinity repressed.

THE ODDLY SHAPED MAN.

> (*To the Discreet Council of Old Gods*)

I stand now before you in the old tradition

To offer a proposal for my split condition.

I labored wretchedly in making my appearance

And I humbly plead your wisdom and forbearance.

The journey you've ordained has revealed the guilt and pain

Of the errant by-paths leading into your domain.

Through them I have sacrificed by own begotten son

To try and make atonement for the things I've done...

But I'll get to the point that you've let me in:

I want your release from the stain of sin.

The ape's body I have borne to reach this place

I've suffered long and worn the signs upon my face.

The lonely steps I took I need not here retrace

Only to appeal to your benevolence and grace.

They were given then as signposts of your winding way;

I've shown you I could bear them as you see me here today.

I fulfilled them as you gave them -- only this have I to ask:

Relieve me of my grief for me to now complete the task

Of re-connecting Nature's song with the world of light

To free the soul once hidden in the darkest night.

It's the only plea within my heart I need convey:

That in your wisdom you see fit to take the guilt away...

A Psychic Chorus

Only the spontaneous production of a symbol by the unconscious is able to reconcile the split between it and the conscious mind -- one of the reasons the old alchemists referred to the attainment of their goal as being possible only with the "consent of God." Jung called it a uniting symbol, and it represents the realization of a psychic reality far beyond the capacity of thought to conceive. The dawning of this deeper sense of reality has always circled around symbols of the sun and light as the emergence of a more diffuse emotional awareness. Here, a slightly Eastern influence reflects the urge to wholeness repressed by the exclusive character of Western patriarchy. It reveals a level of the collective unconscious which is universally common. An historical scholar in his own right, Jung traced the psychological connections between Western religious ideas and those of Eastern philosophy.

You strangers! Hurry forth before the dawn!

See what thing the rising sun has cast its light upon!

From the darkness which for so long was your home

Hasten to the rhythm of the metronome!

Gracious limbs are bowing in the breeze

Tops lit up like ancient Christmas trees.

They now find us knelt on humble knees

For they have fused their music with our pleas.

Take now your place upon the sacred ground

In deepest darkest earthly meditation;

For, all the dark and bitter pain you found

Has turned around today to form elation!

Consider true the penetrating symbols

That long exchanged have brought you to this place.

Feel now your gladdened heart and how it trembles

At the overwhelming mystery of Nature's grace.

See the glowing sky on yonder ocean;

The rosy hue encircling all around

Feel the force of Nature's quiet motion

As from her womb a newborn baby girl is found!

She it was the monster serpent once informed

Hid behind the veil the naked prophet rent.

She it was the ancient Trinity deformed

Before the naked prophet was from darkness sent.

She: the little girl who toppled heaven's throne

And Nature dared conceive her magic all alone!

She from whom the blasphemers fled in fright

Before their monstrous needs were given light!

Now we all are quite astonished just like they

At what Leviathan concealed within his breast:

For, the hallowed image of the Son of Man today

Is become the humble daughter Mother Nature blessed!

THE ANCIENT KING.

He was no man but a striving little god indeed

Bound unwitting to the shadow-lord of Nature's need;

Inspired by the haughty might of intellect

To overcome the only demon it could not detect.

But through years of struggle he was made to understand:

His gods and devils both were under her command.

In his dark retreat there were no songs to sing --

He found no treasured phrases to recite;

No lofty platitudes to which to cling

To turn like magic darkness into light.

But what his worldly fate had then prepared in him

For him to have the strength to call his own --

For drowsy eyes to strain to see through visions dim --

Was Nature's light but hidden like a seedling grown

To birth an image now reflecting her -- and him.

The highest task his lofty intellect achieved

In its lost and lonely god-like imitation

Was the recognition of its own light deceived

When it discovered in the end its limitation.

How unbeknownst his thinking had become a prey

Of the feeling-world it thought it could control!

And how very far it carried him astray

From the earthly forms concealed within his soul!

When a man cannot conceive a thing he calls it chance;

What his intellect cannot perceive is circumstance.

These are gods who weave their way through world events

To create analogies of man's experience.

Such ideas are certainly as old as humankind

And were never the inventions of the conscious mind.

The voices in the darkness always told him this

Though the intellect itself cannot experience --

No matter how it strives to pierce the dark abyss --

The secret symbols hiding in the world of sense.

The dreams I sent released him from the prison

Defining thinking's artificial sphere;

They slowly overtook his world of egotism

To reveal the spirit-functions Life intended here.

He has now the opportunity to enter in

The process of the evolution of the self within.

How truly simple life may seem in retrospect

But how difficult it is to make a man reflect!

How insane was he to think his mind could fight

The power of a god and Nature too?

Yet such is man's peculiar little flight

Through the universe of his subjective view...

Epilogue

The conclusion stresses the psychological knowledge and spiritual reflection needed to accept, as natural balancing functions, the inner images mediating unconscious purposes. It brings into relief the exclusive nature of collective perception and the inability of science and religion as cultural institutions to acknowledge their own rejected opposites. This dark counter-pole informs the individual, through his/her direct emotional experience, of images and ideas that express analogies of the very spirit-life intellect cannot conceive as a result of its rational perspective. We have innate functions which correspond to the irrational factors of circumstance, chance, and accident -- even the probability of science: all express the adaptive nature of psychic energy and its creative flow toward the future. Jung stated it this way: "There are no accidents." The emotional experience of a spiritual power greater than one's own desires opens to an awareness that a profoundly unknown psychic reality is continually striving to fulfill purposes far more extensive than those which conscious will or choice can imagine – the nature of dreams.

THE ODDLY SHAPED MAN.

> The fleeting voices ringing in my dreams before
>
> Have now revealed the passage to the narrow door;
>
> For, the strange emotions they so long ago divined
>
> Were the spirit-functions in my own unconscious mind.
>
> The little infant Nature's hidden womb supported
>
> Was the virgin birth my Christian heritage aborted
>
> Conceived by ancient soul-sparks which glittered in the night
>
> Through distant images in which my own truths burned;
>
> Somehow brought together by reflected light
>
> To feel the depth for which my Christian spirit yearned.

A softer radiance revealed these hidden things

Than the lightning piercing once inside my heart;

And only now from Nature's silent well it springs

To bathe the wound the lightning split apart.

Like Prometheus who to the jagged rocks was chained

Whose gaping wound was healed each night anew --

Only to appear again when daylight reigned --

This mythic darkness heals my spirit too.

Its earthly mystery has brought its meaning near

To the misery which once exceeded fear.

For, the opposites then raging in my mind

Only in this hidden realm may be combined;

And only its creative act release the shame

Hid within in the turbid glow of Spirit's flame...

So many times I asked myself how it could be

I'd labored on so long with such uncanny feeling

Relentlessly creating over half a century

The pieces of the puzzle of my truth revealing;

Though I never fully understood the truth was me

These dissociated notions were concealing.

Yet every time I asked a question it expanded

With a greater query added to its store;

And for each a greater answer was demanded

Always more perplexing than the one before.

The busy corner of my conscious personality

Could not endure this trial and stay the way it was;

For this struggle forced upon me the reality

Of the earthly spirit and the wondrous things it does.

It required of me everything I had and more

To meet the tension of its underworld demand.

It re-created who I thought I was before

And over Time a selfish youth became a man.

I still ask the questions and receive another clue

Though the answers I had long ago expected

Were not to questions from my former point of view;

For, the inquiries my thinking once directed

It took the Inner Man to ask anew...

So I'm humbled by uncertainty and doubt

Holding tightly their creations in my heart;

And I pray another riddle be fetched out

To know the life my thinking rent apart.

For Nature's opposites are mysteries indeed --

They force a man to self-examination;

And their energies create the hidden deed

Only later crying out for explanation.

Each man has this inner wisdom in his soul

But whose small pride will honestly admit it?

Who indeed possesses courage to extol:

This ancient deed was done and *I'm* the one who did it?

I only hope I'm able to forgive myself

For the ignorance I swore upon the youth

Who always saw the sin in someone else

And veiled the contradictions of my own truth.

The black dot of antiquity when it appeared

Before the child whose innocence was torn apart

Contained the living Deity my thinking feared

Yet always lived within my own divided heart.

Whether it was cosmic and described a big-bang blast

For scientists to see in it a mythic vision --

Or whether it alluded to an earthly past

Compelled as compensation for a man's division;

Its core of gravity revealed a mighty girth

And a man is never free from Nature's dreams.

When a Lord rules heaven and a Devil lords the earth

What force is left to mediate the two extremes

But the voice his *inner* nature brings to birth?

That a living force must rule this world I have no doubt;

How it is revealed to other men I cannot say.

I only know the changes my condition brought about

By reflecting on it in my own peculiar way.

My critical evaluations of the world of men

Were less judgmental than the need for separation

From the things obscuring my experience within

Of how this Force revealed to *me* my aberration.

If a man does not discern the myth in him created

By the long-forgotten souls who forged his modern mind

How can he determine through the principles they stated

Which subjective truths to keep and which to leave behind?

The dark seed of sickness is its own demanding goal;

Few of us are spared the pressures of its threat.

But there lies too the process of becoming whole:

No concept of the norm has found the answers yet

To the unknown mystery concealed in every soul.

Many may not feel the need for such concern

Compelling those who seek beyond the status quo;

Yet history is full with those who came to yearn

For something greater than a life tossed to and fro

Between what others taught and what they sought to learn.

To some of you this turn-around may seem insane

As the process did to me I must confess.

But Nature had a purpose in my self-disdain

Not to be concealed beneath collective dress.

The gods I worshiped hid the secret intimations

Of reflections pushed to consciousness' extent;

And in turn these efforts mirrored the relations

With the force below describing its intent.

No man is an island as the saying goes

Nor can a god exist without a man's reflection;

For a god relates a man to what he thinks he knows

To the inner force revealing his direction.

Thus I have been driven by Uncertainty and Doubt

To question my perception of this world of gods and men;

And a hidden nature turned my thinking inside-out

To pose the crazy question back to me again:

If a man reflects a nature who reflects the man

Might not this double-sided nature then in turn

Twice reflect the opposites inherent in its plan

To offer men the things for which their spirits yearn?

A greater pair of opposites conceals the primal force

Yet my interpretation of it yields a smaller pair;

And my subjective thought cannot conceive the source

Of the mystery encircling this earthly square.

This square is meant to orient my mind to Nature's needs --

The only world there is despite the fancy creeds.

The circle of her mystery is found within my soul

And it is there the smaller pair may be made whole.

She rules the inner world a god cannot reveal

But through the medium her fantasies conceal.

Her symbols to the spirit-world as facts are known

For what the world comprises is symbol alone;

No less true today than the time when Goethe wrote it

But still a notion much too strange for men to note it.

Gods once represented this elusive form of thought

But science has destroyed it without a care.

Its literal interpretations since have brought

The very wrath of those old gods to come to bear.

Even if religious men from centuries ago

Were not quite able to discern their evil deeds;

Nor was I nor any man for things he didn't know

Of the errant winding course the Spirit leads.

Yet they held esteem for *something* greater than themselves --

However misconstrued their fantasies had been --

Than the rational contrivance modern thought compels

To evade responsibility for Adam's sin.

It finds us in the greatest peril ever seen

Through the darkest chapters of the most unconscious man;

For the god of Nature modern man sees more obscene

Than any past philosophies the mind could scan.

Further up and on we fly with no care for the past

Nor even for the blinded future we create;

No truth ever sacred to an intellect bound fast

To a hostile inner world its pride would abrogate.

Its hostile nature is reflection of the fear

Of the deeper world opposing man's projection;

Leaving only phantoms of a demon to appear

In the most unconscious forms of self-rejection.

Self-enchantment is a necessary evil --

In youth today as in the history of man --

To protect the mind from forces so primeval

Creation and destruction both are their demand.

These overwhelming powers must be seen apart

From the little man who finds himself between the two

And he must separate their urges in his own heart

Lest his creations lead to his destruction too.

Surely Nature seeks a consciousness for something more

Than the pleasures and diversions we now labor for.

Surely some new image will create a brighter sphere

Than the world of self-indulgence we've created here.

The god of progress has revealed this dark momentum --

Still the young reaction of a fragile consciousness

To the fear of its own thinking's excrementum

And its fertilizing power in the dark abyss.

Were it not for those few giants Nature scattered

Among the rabble of the men who've seized the earth

Nothing of our dark travail will much have mattered

But the light their searching minds have brought to birth:

Goethe, who perceived the soul with clarity and hope;

Nietzsche, who then pierced the darkness of a blacker hole;

Jung, who saw the inner world as through a telescope

And established bases of a science of the soul;

Neumann, who described its evolutionary scale --

These were men who penetrated Spirit's modern veil.

They perceived the changing current humans struggle with

To know the ancient beast who birthed our modern myth.

www.ingramcontent.com/pod-product-compliance
Lightning Source LLC
Chambersburg PA
CBHW080410290526
45791CB00008BA/2215